# Poetry From Behind Mental Walls

## Chris Smith

This book is a sampling of poems I wrote during my time at the mental hospital, Whiting Forensics Hospital (WFH), and during my tenure under the Psychiatric Security and Review Board (PSRB) while in the state of Connecticut. These poems range from entertaining to serious, but were deemed by me to showcase various important things and themes of my life, written with my poetic flare. Personally, I would like to thank you for your interest in my book and the enclosed poems my book showcased. I hope you enjoy these poems as much as I had writing them.

Sincerely,
Chris Smith

# CONTENTS

## Poem #1: New York Giants Beating the Undefeated Patriots in the Superbowl

My New York Giants are the Best!

They beat the Undefeated Patriots in the Superbowl test.

That was the best game I saw in my life.

Late in the fourth quarter, there was a lot of strife,

Because the Patriots got the lead late in the game.

But on a late down Giant's quarterback, Eli Manning, threw a pass that was lame.

Wide receiver, David Tyree, caught the pass that was crude,

And got millions, what a lucky dude!

Then quarterback, Eli Manning threw a pass on par,

That wide receiver, Plexico Burress, caught in the end zone to put the Patriot's hopes for victory too far.

With only three minutes left in the game, the score was too deep,

And the Patriot's fans did weep,

Especially when the Giants defense had Patriot's quarterback, Tom Brady, in a sack,

At that point the Patriots lost all attack.

After the game I called my family,

And much to the surprise of me,

We were all happy and relaxed,

Since the New York Giants gave the New England Patriots the ax.

And the Patriots were 18 and 1 after the Giants won.

It was great to see the Patriot's winning streak was done.

That win was nothing small,

Yet after the victory the Giants could stand tall.

They could stick out their triumphant chest,

Since they earned the title of being the best.

## Poem #2: Ode to Snackie Cakes and Snacks

One snackie cake I like by the pound,
Is a fudgy and chocolate Fudge Round.
One thing I love but would hate to bake,
Is a white chocolate-covered Zebra Cake.
Cherry Cordials are so crazy good,
That I could eat a box but ask, "I should?".
Nutter Butters as far as the eye can see,
Would fill me with jubilee.
Similar are the chocolate coated Star Crunch,
Eaten after a satisfying lunch.
Christmas Tree Cakes at Christmas are great,
White or Milk Chocolate, both are first rate.
Rice Krispie Treats are all I like to eat,
And making them with "extras" cannot be beat.
The cakes with raisins and cream, I see while I dream,
Sure makes my stomach growl and makes my eyes beam.
Like the chocolate and strawberry rolls line up in configuration,
Tastes so awfully good for real and in my imagination.
The chocolate-coated peanut butter filled cookie,
I like to eat, now, as a snack food veteran and when I was a rookie.
Brownies with walnuts or sprinkles I love to eat at home,
Or away on travel when I roam.
Even though I get one chance through life,
Snacks like these lessen my daily strife.
I will eat these until they put me in the ground,
While I eat responsibly so I don't become too round.

## Poem #3: Weight of Work

When I was a young adult I gained a lot of weight,
And to be honest I never had a date.
All the food I used to eat,
I was way past replete.
However, I used to work all the time,
Working so hard it was a crime.
The only thing I used to do leisurely.
Was to play video games and to watch TV.
Also, I go for a drive in my car,
Nowhere special, just to fast food places near and far.
I wish I could have been a more active person all-around,
However, I was addicted to work until I was round.
All I had to do was stop and play,
But for success, all of my work was the price I did pay.
To try and do something meaningful and deep,
Yet all I did was weep.
For all my success I had to atone,
For all those years of being isolated and alone.
The way I was going led to a lot of strife,
And the way I looked and felt, I never had a wife.
Hopefully I can get back on track,
And stop everyday breaking my back.
I just hope it is not too late,
To be happy and to do something great.

## Poem #4: My Little Dachshunds

When I was a young, nine Dachshunds were part of my family,
They were always dear to me.
They had little black and tan chests,
They had a big doghouse where they took their rests.
When I came outside, they would always run,
And playing with them was always fun.
As far as pets go, they were awfully good,
They were as friendly to me as they themselves could.
You always see them wish,
That we would bring them extra food on their dish.
But too much food would impair,
Their wobbly little legs with black and tan hair.
With these little dogs I could relax,
Even when my stress level was to the max.
As for typical dog problems, they never really shed,
We had to just clean up their poop instead.
As for dogs, they're classified as hounds,
You can tell this by how they sniff around their grounds.
In the winter, we brought them in from the cold,
We did not want them to freeze and to see them grow old.
Each one of them were really tame,
And my brothers and I gave each one of them their name.
They got to roam in their yard wild and free,
Just like everyone else in the family.

## Poem #5: Easter Island Obama Man

Easter Island Obama Man had only himself to blame,
He owned the Easter Island statue and Former President Barack Obama pictures from which he got his nickname.
He was deaf in both, not just one ear,
So he could not tell if you are coming near.
But he knew just when to fart,
He had made his release of noxious bodily gas into an art.
When I would watch television, he would sit right next to me,
All-of-a-sudden, he lets one fart free.
It stunk horribly bad because he was lactose-intolerant and drank milk,
So everyone in the room had to smell his ilk.
While we were all "on the run",
He grabbed the television remote and watched what he wanted for fun.
It was not his mental illness; he was just being rude,
But that was his personality…a nasty dude.
However, the hospital had him on transitional leave,
Even with his extremely gross flatulent pet-peeve.
He was just nasty and passive aggressive all around,
Like when he dumped the ice for what he claimed was a coffee ground.
He actually reached in to with his dirty hand and cup to get ice,
And since he was corrected by staff, he dumped it because he wasn't nice.

## Poem #6: Ode to the "Bathroom Man"

The "bathroom man" on our hospital unit was risqué,
He was in the bathroom at least 60% of everyday.
And on the trees he took his toll,
Because he squandered many a paper roll.
And, in one of the few stalls, he took 30 to 45 minutes to go poo,
Without any smell, It made you think, "What did he really do?".
However, if you want to see what was perplexing me,
You will have to come to Dutcher Unit North Three.
It makes you wonder why was he in bathroom so much, what is it all about?
Maybe it was about self-shame and a lot of doubt?
Or maybe it was all the devastation,
That had become of our world and especially our beloved nation?
Or maybe it was simpler than that,
Maybe he had to find security in where he shat?
Or maybe it was about when he was a kid,
Where the bathroom was his safe place where he hid?
Or maybe he could not stand that hospital space,
And for all the time in the bathroom was where he chose to leave his trace?
But for whatever reason and to many people's dismay,
Think of all the time he spent in that bathroom, take up one of the few precious toilets in the one patient's bathroom and getting
in the way.

## Poem #7: Ode to the Forty Year Patient

They held a patient ant the hospital for over forty years, yes they did!
He was committed to the hospital when he was barely more than a kid.
They held him here, excessively, for no good reasons,
Do the math; they held him here for over 160 seasons.
They held him locked up, not to go free,
Even though he was acquitted of a crime on a not guilty plea,
For year after year and day after day,
O'Lord have they made him pay.
They took away more rights and lowered the quality of food,
To the point that it is indigestible and overall rude.
He cannot sleep due to the light,
That peers into his room each and every night.
They took away hours at his patient job, so money he could not make,
All the while, the hospital just kept on the take, take, take.
For all the while, the hospital stole his life,
And replaced it with worsening continuous strife.
The hospital won't let him go, not even now,
They want drive him for their "pound of flesh", like a horse and plow.
From the world, the hospital kept him hid,
Until they can bury him and say, "Good Rid!".

## Poem #8: Ode to the Terrible Roommate

I had a terrible roommate named Pete,
He acted as if his head was full of concrete.
He ranted about not having a wife or kids as if he was crazy,
And he never cleaned up after himself as if he was lazy.
He used to make such a mess,
Did he have any manners? Only you could guess.
He wore clothes over and over, and he stunk,
Especially of cigarettes and body odor, even worse than a skunk.
He always just got in the way,
Walking our small hallway, back and forth, over and over, everyday.
He always asked questions like what was the date,
Even when he had a watch, he was late.
He used to walk outside and wave at the passing cars,
He looked and talked as if he had been way to drunk in way too many bars.
He never combed the hairs on his head,
But he would ask for cigarettes from everyone else instead.
He would yell about his social security being stole in his rant,
Like somebody could get him his money in an instant.
He was always "cheeking" his medications,
So his roommates, including me, had to listen to his crazy self-conversations.
So I can hope you can agree,
That I was happy when he moved away from me.
Because my food he stole and liked to eat,
Hopefully you never have to have a roommate like Pete.

## Poem #9: Ode to the Smokers

Outside I see all the smokers smoke,
Coughing up a lung whenever they smoke.
They always smoke around me even though I don't smoke and want to be left alone,
And I got all their second-hand smoke until I moan.
My grandmother died of emphysema in her house,
She didn't want to see us and died hidden away like a mouse.
She was so ashamed to see her in that way,
This was terrible for us in our dismay.
I see them smoke like chimney,
Wait until they need extra oxygen, then they won't be free.
To live a wonderful life,
The illnesses and money to smoke will lead to constant strife.
Heaven forbid a mother smokes having a kid,
That kid could be disfigured if she did.
Even worse the nicotine and all is an addiction,
Companies' love of money caused this personal affliction.
Cancer can be caused which as of now has no cure,
Even if the smoker lived a good life that was pure.
The cigarettes and cigar wrappers and stubs are pollution,
That ruins our kids' world and nation…that is not a solution.
They buy cigarettes and cigars until they are broke,
I hate seeing their cash and lives literally go up in smoke.

## Poem #10: The Curse of Being Hispanic

For me, it is a curse to be Hispanic,
Just because my dad is from Puerto Rico, shouldn't cause a panic.
People mistreat me because me skin is a little darker than the rest,
They discriminate against me even though I do my best.
The question," Are you Hispanic?", I hate,
When it is asked I get irate.
It is just a way for bigoted people to exclude,
I am accepting of everybody, so I think it is rude.
I don't speak Spanish, not even at my home,
Nor anywhere else that I roam.
My dad tells me to say that I am White,
So I don't have to bear the "Hispanic plight".
In Connecticut, when I answer that I am Hispanic for a job,
The employers quickly take away the position and rob,
Me of a chance even though I have an advanced degree,
Their actions dictate their hatred to my ethnicity.
I should be treated just like any other human,
But ignorance is quick to be used to make me subhuman.
I try to be the best I can be everyday,
Which makes ignorant people live in dismay.
Don't mistreat me like people do to people, who are mentally disturbed or manic,
Just because I happen to be born Hispanic.

## Poem #11: Cog in a Wheel / Ode to Workers Everywhere

They will work you like a cog in a wheel,
They don't care how it makes you feel.
They will work you 20 hours a day,
And only pay you for 40 hours a week and unfairly you don't get your honest pay!
They will ask you for your intellectual property and trust,
That they can exploit it for **their** monetary lust.
They will work you to the bone,
And they will fire you if you moan.
They will try to pay you less and take from you all the time,
Even if they need to hire a lawyer to get away with their crime.
They will try to sound righteous and true,
But they will work you to death and try to screw,
You out of what you deserve for your works,
Because they are just evil maniacal jerks,
Your personal and family life will go to hell,
And they will say, "Oh Well".
They have such a toxic work environment, you want to release,
And fly free like a gaggle of geese.
Yet they will force you to work like a bug getting squished by a heel,
For you are just a cog in a wheel.

## Poem #12: I Prefer Women Who Are Petite, Decent And Have Runner's Builds

Women who are petite and decent with runner's builds I prefer,
I know some other men will have preferences that differ.
Some men prefer women who are fat,
I am just not into that.
Some men love women with muscles "all day",
I don't prefer women that way.
Some men prefer any women even when they act crude,
But I want women who are decent and not rude.
Some men love promiscuous women who like to roam,
But I want a woman that prefers to build a life together and make a home.
Some men prefer women with tattoos all over their bod,
I don't prefer that so I don't give those women another nod.
Some men prefer women with a lot of piercing spots,
Those women just don't give me the "hots".
I think it is the way I was raised,
To be conservative in nature and look for women who are well behaved.
In school, a girl named Teresa fit the bill,
But she was with another guy she later married, much to his thrill.
Rarity determines preferences I heard,
And decent women are rare nowadays and worth every word.
I like to think I like women who are decent and demure,
Those are just the type of women I prefer.

## Poem #13: Lara, The Woman That Got Away

Lara was the woman, who got away,
Every day I regret it to my dismay.
She was so decent, wholesome, cute and sweet,
Just the girl you want to meet.
She had big and beautiful hazel eyes,
Ones that would melt the hearts of most guys.
She was very quiet and demure,
For a guy like me, those characteristics are an allure.
She came from a good family,
This left a big impression on me.
I used, to her, tickle and tease,
Which she put up with for me, for which she was trying to please.
She was conservative but she let me play,
Of which I grew fond of her every day.
Every day we would meet,
I loved everything about her and I could feel the "heat".
However, I was much to young for marriage,
Let alone to accommodate her wish for a baby in a baby carriage.
So I had to let her go,
Not knowing how much it would hurt and now I do know.
I wish I could meet her now and make her stay,
Because I miss what we cherished when I let her get away.

## Poem #14: Ode to the Whiting Forensic Hospital (WFH) Staff

To be a staff at Whiting Forensics Hospital (WFH) must be great,
All you have to do to keep your job is not be late.
Yes, I am saying that with a sarcastic tone,
But how much the staff gets paid, they should not moan.
They can, verbally, give patients a "bunch of crap",
And if the patients complain, the staff can write a bunch of bad notes on the patients – a patient's trap.
All the staff have to say is that the patient is crazy,
To do nothing all day but cause problems and be lazy.
A lot of them yack all day,
And not fulfill patient's requests to the patient's dismay.
Most of the staff don't have the temperament to go to another job and be hired,
But because of their union's strength, the staff won't be fired.
A lot of staff get their "jollies" out of being rude,
To patients who are just trying to live their lives. How Crude!
To most of the staff they treat it as a game,
At the expenses of the patients. What a crying shame!
The staff has the patient's morale broke,
But for fear of bad notes and elongated hospital stays, the patient's views will not be spoke.
Some staff pays certain patients, called "Hitmen", to punch,
Other patients, so they staff can get at the victim patient for the cost of some coffee or a fast food lunch.
The staff loves the pay and the benefits given by the state,
On top of that they get to "piss off" patients, sadistically speaking, being a staff must be great.

## Poem #15: My Family Cat Named Bears

My family had a cat named Bears,
She was a magician's cat with jet black hairs.
Except for a patch of white hair on her chest,
We called it her "soul patch" in jest.
She used to hiss,
And when she attacked you leg, she would never miss.
She used to jump on my dad when he was asleep,
My dad used to yell, "Ow!", because her claws went in so deep.
"Kibble Fish" was her nickname,
Because she loved that dry food, all the same.
She also liked sandwich meat,
And she would eat it until she was replete.
Past that she was finicky and was picky,
She did not eat anything she thought was icky.
When I first met her, she was small enough to fit in my hand,
We dressed her up like she was in a rock band.
With pants, shirt and beret on her head,
She would not have it and made us take it off of her instead.
She was part of the family,
And we let her, in the house and yard, run free.
She was a "mouser" and on mice she preyed,
That was how, for the family, she paid.
With the family, we had good times and that cat we showed our cares,
For our family cat named Bears.

## Poem #16: Connecticut, The Wannabe State

Connecticut is a wannabe state,
If you want services, indefinitely you have to wait.
Their state government is modeled after the U.S. Congress,
But they cannot get anything done, as I digress.
Connecticut has its own channel on TV,
But it is used for the state to insist on self for its own ego, between you and me.
Connecticut people have such an ego,
They are just miserable people, especially try and be a person with, so they should let the chip on their shoulder go.
The state likes to spend more money than it can raise via tax,
Deficits are what the state runs, its just the facts.
Connecticut tries to prop-up its restaurants and food,
But almost no food television shows come to this state because its food services are so crude.
This state's capital, Hartford, wants to be like Boston or New York City,
But in all facets it just isn't, what a pity!
Connecticut cannot even keep a professional team of sports,
Every team that has tried to come to Connecticut did so poorly, those teams told the state to "Eat their shorts!".
The cops and legal systems in Connecticut are so bad today,
Those citizens are leaving the state "in droves" and prospective future citizens are deciding to stay away.
The data says Connecticut is not a place for the elderly and old,
No good senior services and high taxes await the elderly bold.
This state tries to be something it is not,
A respectable state, understandably its reputation is shot.
I won't lie, wannabes are people and things I hate,
Just like the people and things associated with this state.

## Poem #17: Hair, Hair, Everywhere

My body grows a lot of hair,
I shed here, there, and everywhere.
I grow tons of hair on my appendages including my pairs of leg and arm,
If there wasn't hair there, my diabetes might be bad enough to do bodily harm.
I shed hair all over the floor,
Every time I sweep it up there is more.
When I shave, there is hair all over the sink,
It clogs the drain that is hard to clean, what a fink!
Having excessive hair is considered crude,
Especially on the face where food gets in it…how rude!
All that hair I have to shave,
Because in polite society, that is how you are supposed to look and behave.
Even when anybody towels off, hair comes off of someone,
Especially me, so cleaning all of it up is no fun.
Wouldn't a better hair cleaning device be great?
But for me, that invention would be late.
Because there is so much that comes off of me, due to my dad's side of the family tree.
However, I guess for me using this new invention would be smart,
To just clean the excessive hair and do my part.
For I should take even more extra care,
To clean up my excessive shedding of hair.

## Poem #18: Ode to the Parks

I love to go explore a park,
I used to go there for my morale, to leave a positive mark.
Like the time I went to clean up the trail,
And I had to clean up the fallen branches after hail.
We had to clean up the trails from being in disarray,
I was used to this being a Boy Scout of America, the B.S.A.
I used to put up a tent and set-up camp,
Even when it was raining and the ground was damp.
I even, in the park's lake, we fished,
I wanted to catch a "big one", I wished.
I used to go and plant quite a few tree,
Because I wanted to explore the wild and be free.
I used to camp all night and day,
And do everything I enjoyed without any dismay.
There was so much space and nobody was rude,
Everybody was there to enjoy nature and not be lewd.
There were many times we stayed overnight,
And we would tell stories by the campfire light.
That was when I was young in age,
Now technology, and not nature, is all the rage.
People use to go see birds like a lark,
You can still experience what I say at a neighborhood park.

## Poem #19: I Loved My Fan

I absolutely loved my fan,
All night it ran.
I can sleep well with the sound,
Did I mention my fan was black and round?
I loved all the background noise,
When I slept, to keep my daily poise.
Sometimes I ran it during the day,
Because I was hot and sweaty after the sports I would play.
It had three speeds that it could go,
To regulate if I wanted more or less air flow,
I aimed it, in the summer, at my bed,
But lower on my bed so it didn't blow a lot on my head.
The nice sound and air would make me feel great,
Especially when I slept late.
This fan was a gift from my dad,
When it arrived, I was glad,
Because my previous fan was used so much it had broke,
So it was hard to sleep and I easily awoke.
With that new fan I got a lot of rest,
So I could wake up and do my best.
Being productive was important for me as a man,
That was why I cherished the sleep I got due to my fan.

## Poem #20: Ode to Pizza Toppings

I can eat pizza everyday,
Especially with my choice of pizza toppings to have my pizza my way.
Pepperoni makes my pizza great,
I can have a pepperoni pizza at any time and date.
Sausage is a favorite of my family,
Especially when it is close to being grease-free.
Mushrooms have an interesting taste,
They are so good on pizza, I don't let them go to waste.
Onions are my favorite vegetable on a pizza dish,
I would get it as a pizza topping because it is delish.
Extra cheese on my pizza never gets old,
Even when I have the pizza the next morning when it is cold.
Hawaiian pizza has ham, pineapple and bacon,
It is one of me "go-tos", when pizza I am "a achin'".
Garlic on my pizza, I say, "Yes Please!",
 It is almost as important as the cheese.
Clams on a pizza, in my book, make the pizza taste go far,
It makes the pizza taste go way past par.
Peppers on pizza I like to have for lunch,
I t is a good vegetable to munch.
I eat my pizza toppings and then the crust when I eat pizza my way,
For I would love to eat pizza like that everyday.

## Poem #21: Ode to Superpowers

Superpowers would be great for a girl or guy,
Try and better this world with superpowers is at least, what I would try.
Invulnerability is the power I like most,
So you don't find yourself dead or end up like toast.
Flying would be great so I can be free,
So I can quickly save good people like my family.
Firing bolts of energy would be good,
I would use them to disable bad guys because I should.
Mind reading and influencing would be used to get in a bad guy's head,
So they would do good things instead.
Claws and blades are good to rip and tear,
Just as long as I don't destroy things beyond repair.
Talking to animals would be good to get more,
Information, as long as the animal's conversation are not too much of a bore.
Having steel or harden skin would be good in a fight,
It can keep you in a fight longer day or night.
It could be useful to run fast or stop time,
So you can easily thwart any crime.
Being able to move things with your mind,
Would make a villain able to defeat you hard to find.
Doing good deeds, some people would wonder why,
Because you are a decent and good girl or guy.

## Poem #22: Fast Food Places I Know

I went to a lot of fast food places in my day,
I could get the food I want, right away.
McDonalds Fries and Filet-O-Fish,
Are two delights I want on my dish!
Wendys Junior Bacon Cheeseburger were only a buck,
I could get a few of them…what luck!
Burger King always had the coupons and the deals,
So we could get cheap, good, and filling meals.
Arbys, I love their sandwich, Beef and Cheddar,
I love them so much I don't think they could be any better.
Roy Rodgers, when I was a kid, had a breakfast buffet,
I used to get as much as I want and fill my tray.
Subway had the five dollar footlongs I like,
It was more than I could eat when I was a little tyke.
Chick-Fil-A had chicken nuggets I adore,
That and the waffle fries filled me up so I could not fit through the door.
Long John Silvers' hushpuppies were the best,
That and their fish just blew away the rest.
Taco Bell had chalupas, tacos, and fiesta potatoes for a snack,
It was so yummy it made me go back.
Hardees had an omelet sandwich I liked to munch,
But it was only for breakfast, so I had to head there before lunch.
KFC had chicken that was extremely good,
I would ask myself if I wanted more, and I said, "I would!".
Popeyes chicken sandwich and sides I like to eat,
They were so tasty, they could not be beat.
Yes, fast food places. More I might have to pay,
But the food was so fast and convenient, I could have it all day.

## Poem #23: Be a Better Man

In retrospect, I should have been a better man,
From having a relationship with a significant other, I ran.
I used video games and television not to care,
It got so bad I didn't even comb my hair.
On top of that I gained a lot of weight,
From eating unhealthy and, everyday, working from morning to late.
I would eat all the time and, additionally, have specific meals like lunch,
And having greasy and fatty meals, I used to munch.
I did not want to be rejected, that I did dread,
I stayed away from relationships instead.
From more malicious and nasty women, I worried, would prey,
On my good nature and, essentially, take advantage of me so I stayed away.
So I had low self-esteem and wondered why,
Women would always choose another guy.
Trying to get a woman to date was such a quest,
Because the ones I went for me were "gold diggers" and not the best.
I wanted a female companion, who was decent and well-spoken,
But most of them were trashy and verbally attacked me until inside I was broken.
It became hard to date a female stranger,
Because I worried that they were using me and I was in danger.
All I wanted to find was "the one",
But I am older and I don't think I will find that special someone.
I am still a good person and hope for a mate I will not can,
Because I will always try to be a better man.

## Poem #24: Sodas, Soda I like to Drink

There are many sodas I like to drink,
At every meal I drank them, they were the common link.
Coca Cola was sugary and sweet,
It was a great soda to beat the summer heat.
Diet Pepsi was a good drink for a meal,
It was a good soda without sugar and had a satisfying appeal.
Diet Dr. Pepper was a soda I could drink every day,
"It had a unique flavor!", some people say.
Sprite was a tasty soda that was clear,
But it was so good; I could drink it and make it disappear.
Diet Mountain Dew was a flavorable soda that I liked,
I used to drink the non-diet brand when I was a little tyke.
A soda I liked in college was Surge,
When I needed the energy and caffeine I drank it when I got the urge.
Ginger Ale calmed my stomach when it was uneasy,
It tasted good and it stopped me from feeling queasy.
Orange Soda, my favorite one was Crush,
I would drink that and enjoy it by not drinking it in a rush.
Grape Soda was so good I wished it would come back,
And have it with meals or a tasty snack.
Barque's Root Beer had a very desirable spice,
When I drank it, it made me feel nice.
I could drink 7-Up until it hurt,
My brother, had its slogan, "Make Seven, Up Yours", on his shirt.
Cream Soda, I used to drink when I wanted to relax,
Because I enjoyed its flavor to the max.
If I was served a meal, I would think the host a fink,
If he or she did not serve a soda to drink.

## Poem #25: Whiting Forensic Hospital (WFH)

Patients at Whiting Forensic Hospital (WFH) are essentially in jail,
They even have police officers opening their mail.
WFH is supposed to be a hospital for mental health,
But they hold patients there to charge the state and get monetary wealth.
The food is bland, especially at lunch,
Patients try to get their families to send personal snacks for something tasty to munch.
The staff tries to antagonize patients everyday,
But if a patient acts up, a heavy price he or she will pay.
Patients are not supposed to be "doing time",
Because most were not guilty by reason of mental defect for a crime.
The treatment teams try to write reports that are bad,
I stopped reading those reports, so I didn't get mad.
Trying to sell the public that patients are dangerous is their game,
But for people in the know, know that is a money-making excuse that is lame.
The psychiatric medications the hospital gives makes patients gain weight,
And make patients have health problems the hospital "catches" too late.
Patients have no real legal resource for problems to be publically spoken,
So the patients' morale is irreparably broken.
Many patients are so institutionalized, due to overlong incarcerations, that they won't try,
They won't try to get out and stopped asking, "Why?".
WFH holds patients too long to see them fail,
Because these patients are being held against their will in a psychiatric jail.

## Poem #26: Ode to Breakfast Foods

Breakfast has its own stereotypical food,
When you smell it cooking its gets you in the "eating mood".
Cereal, hot or cold,
Has so many different flavors it never get old.
Bacon is a meat I love to have on my dish,
It is so well liked that vegetarians mostly cheat with bacon, even for bacon they wish.
Toast, I like those crunchy pieces of bread,
I like it better than other options I could have instead.
Pancakes are good with maple syrup and butter,
"I want more than three!", are the words I would utter.
Eggs I like scrambled with cheese,
But I really like them hard-boiled and when asked to have them I say," Yes please!".
Hashbrowns are nice and crunchy on my plate,
When they are served for breakfast, I don't want to be late.
Ham, I like cut thick by the pound,
I like it nice and grilled on my plate that happens to be round.
Homefries are good when mixed with cheese onions and stuff,
When I get it, there always seems to be more than enough.
Sausage is good as a patty or link,
But it will be gone and eaten in a hurry if you blink.
Waffles, right out of the toaster, I like to eat,
With butter, fork, and knife until I am replete.
French toast, with cinnamon and sugar, packs a great punch,
It is so good, I like it a bunch.
You can have breakfast all day if you want if you're a lucky dude,
Because breakfast is a mindset as well as the characteristic food.

# Poem #27: Living Under the Psychiatric Security and Review Board (PSRB)

Living under the PSRB, everything is open and shut,

They always" paint" the patient in the worst light, no matter what.

As a patient you have to watch what you do and say,

Because the PSRB will twist it to look bad on a patient, all the way.

You have to watch when your roommate cooks lunch,

Because he could leave the stove on, and if anything happens, the patient will get in trouble, a bunch.

If you as a patient try to fill out a grievance sheet,

The PSRB will "villanize" the patient and the grievance will be used to in the patient's stop a patient's discharge, the patient's personal defeat.

The PSRB will withhold a patient's release,

So the patient cannot live and fly free, like a gaggle of geese.

The PSRB will try everything to make a patient's life a nightmare,

While the state is paying the PSRB personnel's salary. Why should they care?

The PSRB has, over the patient, the power of the pen and paper,

To make the patient look devious and malicious in any alleged caper.

It doesn't matter how good the patient is all-around,

The PSRB will manipulate the patient's life until he or she is in the ground.

With all the PSRB's restrictions on patients, we cannot relax,

And any PSRB-perceived slight by the patient, makes problems for the patient to the max.

The PSRB holds patients at institutions and in the community for way too long,

 But if a patient speaks up, the PSRB will report the patient in the wrong.

They test patients all the time for doing drugs,

Even if drug use is not in their history. The PSRB treats the patients as if they were drug-using thugs.

The PSRB will tell a patient if he or she has a problem, "We should talk",

Since the PSRB will negatively talk about the patient. Instead the patient should just go for a walk.

For patients, living under the PSRB is like being stuck in a rut,

The PSRB owns you and has no real overseeing entities to be responsible to, so keep your mouth shut.

## Poem #28: Ode to Football Positions

Football at our family's house and in our country is an institution,
With specialized athletes at every position.
The safeties cover passes "over the top",
And if a runner or pass catcher tries to get past them, they give them a "pop".
The offensive line is the offensive backfield's shield,
So the offense can pass or run all over the field.
The quarterback is the one in charge,
He is the "general on the field" and "living large".
The defensive line gives pressure up front,
And trying to sack the quarterback, they are always on "the hunt".
The linebacker is behind the defensive line,
The can tackle the running back and blitz the quarterback just fine.
The kicker is the one that kicks the ball,
And gets extra points and field goals, so without them the team would fall.
The running back is getting yards by being on the attack,
Teams need a good one, not just another athlete "off the rack".
The wide receiver catches the pass,
Teams need an athlete with endurance and stamina, so they don't run "out of gas".
The punter is the player that determines field position on a fourth down,
Pinning an opponent's team deep on their side of the field is good for a team all-around.
The cornerback picks up a receiver "on the go",
To stop an opponent teams scoring and keep their offensive yards low.
A tight end catches the balls "over the middle",
And they block with the rest of the offensive line, so they are not little.
All these positions are important and need to be filled with the right athletes that can fulfill their team's reputation.
To build their team's dynasties in this fine institution.

# Poem #29: Ode to the Handshake

Due to COVID-19, handshakes are now going away,
But when I was young they were in their "heyday".
I used to handshake people that I meet,
It was a formal way for men to greet.
I was told to shake a hand solid and firm,
But not too strong or the other person might squirm.
A handshake with a limp hand was called a "limp fish",
It felt weird as a handshake, so I never liked it and hoped people would stop that handshake, I wish.
"Double pumping" or a second squeeze was done by the old,
I always thought, "Oh!", whenever an elder felt so bold.
Young people used to do multiple handshake maneuvers on TV,
It meant you were part of the club, their family.
Due to COVID-19, nobody wants a handshake touch,
So they "handshake" with their foot very much.
It must be weird at the end of an interview for a job,
Because, in my day, no handshake meant the job position, the company, would rob.
And what about church, when you said, "Peace be with you"?
Due to no contact, no handshakes meant something new to do.
Handshakes amongst friends comes from the heart,
But due to COVID-19, calling from a telephone would be considered "more smart".
I always thought handshakes were here to stay,
But I was wrong, now they are history and are going away.

## Poem #30: My Room is My Safe Place

My room is my safe place,
Where all the negative things I try to erase.
I go there to daydream and play,
Away from people who bring me dismay.
I go there to my private room,
Where danger does not loom.
I go there to lay down my head,
To daydream about fantastic quests while laying down in my bed.
There I can fight monsters and fly,
Or be the heroic and stoic guy.
I don't have to be around people who would shun,
And have make-believe adventures that are fun.
I don't have to see people who give me attitude,
For these people are banned from my room because they are rude.
I can be "king of the mountain" and always the best,
Or be the "life of the party" because of how I jest.
I can go to the farthest expanses of the universe and roam,
While being in my room at home.
My room is where I can go to atone,
When somebody wrongs me, in my room alone.
I can ponder a mystery or do something "deep",
I can do that in my room and not say a peep.
I can get out of the human "rat race",
And come to my room, my own private place.

## Poem #31: Video Games of My Past

I played a lot of video games in my past,
I used to enjoy them and have a blast.
Super Mario Brothers was my first,
Level 8-1 was really long, and with a time limit, was the worst.
The last game I played was Skyrim with an open world,
I liked its action and how the game unfurled.
Borderlands had a great story and had many a gun,
Shooting up the bad guys and beating different areas was fun.
Civilization was a turn-based game and fun to play,
I could literally sit down and play it all day.
Worms Armageddon put a team of worms to kill,
Using weapons like a bazooka made killing the other team's worms a thrill.
Might and Magic, you use different mythical races to make an army to fight,
The skill of blocking up the opponent's archers is inherently right.
Ashtung Spitfire makes you fight in a plane from above,
Getting behind a plane and shooting it down is a sight I love.
Contra was a game that everybody knew the 30 extra life cheat code,
While shooting enemies with the spread gun, they were mowed.
Delta Force, everybody used a SAW as a sniper weapon to have the most kills and be the "top" guy,
"One shot, one kill" was just not going to fly.
10 yard fight was a football game,
For its time, the Artificial Intelligence of the computer was good and not lame.
Pokémon Stadium I used Snorlax to beat Parasect,
In the final battle, to get the highest level Pokémon trophy, as I reflect.
Diablo and Diablo 2, you killed enemies for money and better loot,
And to get your experience and skill levels higher, to boot.
I played my video games hard and beat them fast,
But that was when I was younger, quite a few years in the past.

## Poem #32: A Plethora of Chicken Wing Flavors

Chicken wings with many distinct flavors I love to eat,
They are my favorite chicken meat.
Buffalo flavor is good, tried and true,
It pairs very well with cheese of blue,
Teriyaki flavor is yummy and cool,
I get teriyaki wings when I eat hotter wings, if you don't, then you're a fool.
Spicy sesame ginger flavor is tasty and great,
I just cannot eat too many or I will gain weight.
Mango Habanero flavor is sweet and spicy,
It goes well with a drink of milk that is nice and icy.
Honey flavor is nice and sweet,
It glazes the chicken wing with a flavor that cannot be beat.
Barbeque (BBQ) flavor gives the chicken wing a delightful tang,
You have to eat BBQ wings quick or they will be gone in a bang.
Caribbean jerk flavor, I like a lot but when it is not too hot,
Or after I eat them my taste buds are shot.
Garlic Parmesan flavor, you can never go wrong,
When my friends go out for these wings, I always "tag along".
Siracha wings have a distinct flavor,
And they are not so hot, so you don't have to sign a medical waiver.
Strawberry jalapeno flavor, tastes like the flavors in the name,
Not having ordered enough of these wings is a shame.
Spicy garlic flavor, I like to lick my fingers,
Because this flavor "sticks to you" and lingers.
Honey mustard flavor, I used to have when I was a kid,
When my dad asked if I like it, I replied, "Yes I did!".
Chicken wings and their many flavors cannot be beat,
When the mood for spicy, sweet, or other flavors arises, wings are the best to eat.

## Poem #33: The Country Named "The Best"

If I founded a country, I would name it "The Best",
As the name implies, it would be better than all the rest.
When I am at the United Nations, and called on to speak,
All the other countries would be quiet and meek.
Other countries would be jealous and want to attack,
But better countries would ally with me and have my back.
"The Best Of" would be the name of the capitol seat,
Citizens of "The Best of, The Best" the other countries would have to repeat.
Everybody in "The Best" would not be in danger,
Because the whole country would know each other and not be a stranger.
"The Best" would take care of its elderly old,
So knowledge and wisdom can be passed down and their stories be told.
Younger citizens would be encouraged to learn,
And ignorance and stupidity, our society would spurn.
"The Best" citizens would have a big heart,
And do their best to help each other and do their part.
We would work together to get business done,
And have time to relax and have fun.
It would take a lot of good people to operate this land,
It takes a specific type of earnest people or the country would disband.
To be "The Best" in character and name would not be a jest,
But it takes a lot of commitment by its people to be "The Best".

## Poem #34: Avengers in the Movies

Avengers have been in a lot of movies today,
These movies were so memorable, for my generation, they will be here to stay.
Captain America wears the red, white and blue,
Using his shield to help batter bad guys to save people like me and you.
Ironman had an assault suit and was a genius guy,
He even perfected his suit against icy build-up when he flied extra high.
War machine was a soldier who fought in an assault suit at his best,
But his leg got crippled when he crashed during a quest.
Thor was the god of lightning and could fight,
Using a magical hammer to focus his might.
Hulk was a big brute who liked to smash,
He was a heavy assaulter who used his brawn to bash.
Hawkeye fought with arrows and a bow,
He was always accurate and knew where the arrows needed to go.
Black Widow was an assassin with gadgets so great,
That she took down many bad guys that were extremely irate.
Scarlet Witch had a ton of red power,
That she could help her fellow Avengers in need at any hour.
Vision was created from an infinity stone,
Where he got his power that he always tried to hone.
Black Panther was bestowed power at his Wakanda home,
He took that power to do good things wherever he would roam.
Spiderman got his power from a radioactive spider and was a kid,
He was mentored by Ironman for all the good he did.
Antman could turn small,
And hit bad guys so hard they felt like they hit a wall.
Together they were strong, nobody could stand in their way,
And the movie producers are still making Avengers movies today.

## Poem #35: People Look Best From a Medium Distance Away

People look best from a medium distance away,
This is what I heard a comedian say.
This statement makes sense to me,
Because otherwise they are too close or too far away to see.
If they are too close, you see all the blemishes on someone,
Which makes them unattractive to look at and that is no fun.
If they are too far away and the distance too long,
You cannot see them well and their face or body could be all wrong.
You cannot tell if they are too elderly or old,
You might be attracted to somebody "put out to pasture" and with "mold".
You cannot tell if they are too young at life,
This could get you in trouble and "jammed up" with their strife.
You cannot tell, if they are too far away, if they have a nice face,
You might get too close and they might have a face that looks like it was hit by a medieval mace.
But if you see a person from medium distance you can get a good reference frame,
And if that person looks good, you can get there name.
If you see a person very good,
You can determine if you want to say, "Hi!", or if you should?
From medium distance, you can also hear their words that they have spoken,
To augment their attractiveness with words spoke unbroken.
If you don't get a medium distance reference, it might then be too late,
To back out if the other person isn't that great.
It might be too flakey and superficial just, on looks, to have to stay,
A far distance from a person, but "discretion is the better part of valor" so stay well away.

## Poem #36: McDonalds Sandwiches I Craved

Especially when I was young, McDonalds sandwiches I craved,
To get their sandwiches, money I saved.
Their hamburgers were on special for 29 cent,
I would eat so many I felt like I should have repent.
Their Big Mac had a special sauce and patties of two,
There were so yummy, when I ate them, I would hardly chew.
A Filet-O-Fish would make my day,
Especially when they were on special, I would gladly pay.
The McRib was great with its barbeque sauce,
The sauce was so thick and tangy, it was the boss.
Double Cheeseburgers used to be a buck,
To get burgers like that for a dollar, what luck!
The McChicken was a little spicy,
And went well with a soda, nice and icy.
Big 'N Tasty was a sandwich I liked in the past,
The big burger and vegetables…it was good even though it did not last.
Quarter Pounders used to make me full,
That much burger and the onions with condiments, I thought that burger was cool.
Sausage McMuffins, I loved to eat,
I would eat them at breakfast until I was replete.
Egg McMuffins had Canadian bacon for taste,
I would order these sandwiches with great haste.
The Sausage Biscuit sandwich was so darn good,
I always wanted another, but asked, "I should?".
Chicken Biscuit sandwiches, I got later as an adult,
Why I didn't try them earlier was all my fault.
McDonalds sandwiches, boy, I raved,
Because these were the sandwiches for which I craved.

## Poem #37: Social Workers at Whiting Forensic Hospital (WFH) Liked to Lie

Social Workers at Whiting Forensic Hospital (WFH) liked to lie,
Honestly, I always wondered why.
Wouldn't it be better just to do the work?
Instead of leading a patient on like a despicable jerk!
If a patient says something, the social worker will write something bad,
In the patient's treatment plan, to try to get the patient mad.
The social workers just lead the patient along,
With the patient thinking everything is progressing, yet the patient is wrong.
I just wish the social workers would have just a little heart,
And do their job to help the patient or, plainly, just do their part.
But the social workers don't care and just do their time,
And the patients get held punitively even though they were not guilty by reason on mental defect for a crime.
The social workers can do what they please with the power of the pen and paper,
And hold the patients in limbo, they are the victims of the social worker's caper.
Seeing how the social workers "work" is just a jest,
Because they rather bamboozle the patients than do their best.
I just wish the social workers would get their work done,
But I guess manipulating and controlling patients is just more fun.
For a patient, a social worker you don't want to hound,
Because they will let you rot in the hospital until the patient is six feet in the ground.
As a patient, to the social workers, you don't want to say a peep,
Because the patients are at their mercy and the social workers make "speaking-up" patients weep.
In the end, I wish the social workers would try,
But the truth is they don't, they just rather lie.

## Poem #38: Ode to the "Cemetery Discharge"

A "cemetery discharge" is when a patient has to die,

To get out of Whiting Forensic Hospital (WFH) and the Psychiatric Security and Review Board (PSRB), and I wonder why.

Why do they hold a patient so long?

Even the statutes say not to hold a patient punitively, so what they are doing is wrong!

But it is their system and they know just what to say,

To hold patients indefinitely and the patient's freedom of which they prey.

The only way some patients leave the system is 6 feet in the ground,

With no freedom or voice of freedom to be found.

Not even the patient's family,

Is able to help their relative to get out and that offends me.

Some patients only way to regain freedom is in their eternal sleep,

Without being able to fend for themselves, not even a peep.

A "cemetery discharge" is their only release,

So hopefully in heaven they can find some freedom and peace.

Their only freedom from the WFH and PSRB systems comes when they are dead,

Because the systems preys off them monetarily for its existence instead.

These systems are a bunch of murders and should be charged with a crime,

For stealing the patients' lives, liberty, and happiness by taking away their freedom for a lifetime.

These systems just go on and take another patient's life,

And doesn't care how much it costs the patients' strife.

These WFH and PSRB systems don't care if they take another girl or guy,

It is sad that there are "cemetery discharges" and for a patient to obtain his or her freedom that he or she must die.

## Poem #39: Garden Vegetables I Grew

When I was younger, I grew gardens with my family,
So a love of gardening and a "green thumb" was bestowed on me.
Cucumbers grew all over the place,
They grew so fast you thought the vegetables were in a race.
Tomatoes we grew were big and small,
We had to tie the plants to sticks they grew so tall.
Potatoes they grew in the ground,
We had to dig them out of a little mound.
Onions, we grew and then cooked, were very sweet,
They went well with a burger, what a treat!
Peppers we grew were not too hot,
Because we couldn't enjoy the hot ones due to our tastebuds being shot.
Lettuce, it was hard to grow a perfect head,
But we did well growing them and they did not go bad or end up dead.
Zucchini was good right out of the garden when roasted,
"I cook very good zucchini!", I have boasted.
Pumpkins are very good to grow,
They yield a pretty good crop, if the seeds you know how to sow.
Squash, when roasted in the oven, are good for lunch,
They grow plentiful so you have a bunch.
Green beans grow fast, so you have to pick them almost every day,
We got so many green beans we had to give some away.
Green peas are tasty right out of the garden and out of its shell,
But getting them out of their pods is a lot of work, I do tell.
As an adult, I also found it is not hard,
To grow the vegetable, Swiss chard.
It is rewarding to grow a garden and to see,
The fruits of your labor and to feed the family.

## Poem #40: Laundry, the Scourge of Modern Times

Laundry is just a menace you have to do every day,

It is a chore that is the scourge of modern day in every way.

It is required that your clothes are clean,

They have to be perfect, with no imperfections, and pristine.

The bother of every piece of clothing you have to fold,

All the hours of endless work that goes untold.

For laundry soap and other laundry necessities you have to go to the store,

In order to keep doing this endless chore.

It is a lot easier if the washer and dryer are in the home,

Or you have to drag everything to a Laundromat and have to roam.

Heaven forbid you get something on you during lunch,

Especially if it is ketchup, for that you need to pretreat and use a detergent with "punch".

To spend all those hours, all the time,

Doing a menial chore like laundry, is a crime.

Especially if you have to do laundry for a family,

It is endless and seems you never will be free.

On top of clothes, there are other things like the sheets for your bed,

I would rather be at work doing something productive instead.

When I am doing laundry I want to do something fun,

But I have to wait until the washer and dryer are done.

Having to do laundry just to do it again is so lame,

It just insists on itself like its some kind of game.

However, having to do tons of laundry is the only way,

To like a decent person, you just begrudgingly do it every day.

## Poem #41: Connecticut Legal Rights Project (CLRP)

Connecticut Legal Rights Project (CLRP) was useless for me,

Because I was at Whiting Forensic Hospital (WFH) under the Psychiatric Security and Review Board, the PSRB.

The flagrant abuse of patient's rights by WFH and the PSRB was a complete mess,

And the CLRP lawyer at Dutcher building said he was going to do less.

I had to stop myself from saying, "How can you do less than zero?"!

Needless to say CLRP and their lawyer was not my hero.

CLRP people said PSRB patients signed their life away,

So CLRP let PSRB patients "pay their own price", alone they would have to pay.

CLRP was supposed to uphold the patients' rights,

But they were all talk and not put up any serious legal fights.

They were "paper tigers" that had no real "punch",

While the WFH and PSRB crushed the patients' rights with a "crunch".

CLRP was used by the Department of Mental Health and Addiction Services (DMHAS) so DMHAS could put on paper,

That DMHAS were giving patients legal help to perpetrate a false sense of compassion for their money-grab caper.

CLRP used to help civil patients have peace,

But PSRB patients could not get that until their eventual release.

CLRP is a copout and, for PSRB patients, a shame,

For the patients are victims and used to get state money for WFH and the PSRB in their monetary game.

CLRP's "services" are just a jest,

Who takes up money and a spot for services that the patients need from the best.

The patients need a real "crackshot" lawyer group; you know, an ace,

Not CLRP, who is just there taking up space.

The patients need a lawyer or legal group that has a "pair",

Not CLRP, who for the PSRB patients, they don't care.

Getting better legal help would make patients live better and free,

But not with CLRP, who has done nothing to help PSRB patients, like me.

## Poem #42: Good Guys Finish Last

Ever heard the line, "Good Guys Finish Last"?
It is not just an expression from the past.
I try to do right by everybody every day,
But on my good morals some pathologically-wrong people prey.
They want to see me fall,
To them it's just a game, like a kid with a ball.
I try to help people and be decent in my life's quest,
However, some people "try me" and to their friends they jest.
I do the best I can to help everyone and not be lewd,
All I get from others is attitude.
I try to help everyone all-around,
Even when their aren't good people to be found.
People are quick to shy away from me and call me a "creep",
But I am a good guy and say nothing, not even a peep.
I try to help others, even a stranger,
But I have to watch out for ulterior motives, for I am in danger.
I am good-natured and try to do what is right,
But more manipulative people hate me, so I am in for a fight.
So generous of myself to others I gave,
But I should have realized most other people I cannot redeem and save.
I should do for myself instead,
And all these bad people's problems I should shed.
For them, my empathy and help is just a game,
They were taking advantage of my goodness, what a crying shame!
For these people will, for their jollies, cause me strife,
And antagonize me my entire life.
I have to realize that I am in a different caste,
For decent people like me just won't last.

## Poem #43: Foods I Associate With Summertime

There are foods that I associate with summertime, why?
Because they remind me of my favorite holiday, the 4th of July.
Hamburgers off the grill, I say, "Yes Please!",
Especially if you top them with bacon and cheese.
Hot dogs are great with ketchup, onions, and relish on a bun,
They are portable, so you can walk around and eat to continue your fun.
Barbeque chicken has a great sauce with a zany tang,
When you serve it to everyone, they are gone in a bang.
Baked beans are a good side dish food,
You just have to not pass gas that would be rude.
Potato salad is creamy and great,
You just cannot eat too much or you will gain weight.
Apple pies with smaller chunks of apple are the best,
And it is a symbol of our country, so I keep it "near to the chest".
Tuna salad is good on bread,
It s packed with protein and I use mayonnaise, not cheese, instead.
Macaroni salad has a right place,
As a tasty side dish whatever the case.
French fries are good crunchy and not broken,
I like them skinny and golden brown, so I have spoken.
Ice cream is good in a bowl or a cone,
I can eat so much ice cream my head and stomach start to hurt, and I start to moan.
Grilled cheeses are simple to make and are good,
I love them at a summer cookout. Would I like another? Yes I would!
Egg salad I love to have for a summer lunch,
With potato chips in the sandwich, this packs a crunch.
I think I will eat these foods for summer until I die,
Because these foods are the foods that define summertime for me, that is why.

## Poem #44: Ode to Pie

Oh how I loved to eat pie,
Here were some of my favorite flavors, I won't lie!
Pecan pie was my absolute favorite with its filling gooey and sweet,
I always got it at the grocery store, it couldn't be beat.
Apple pie was great with ice cream on top,
The spices used in the filling added to the ice cream, really made the pie "pop".
Lemon meringue pie had a filling that was tart,
The sturdier meringue part made it look like a work of art.
Lemon pie alone was good and made me pucker,
It was really tart and I "chased" it down with a lollipop sucker.
Key lime pie had a unique flavor,
It is a taste I thoroughly enjoyed and that I savor.
Peach pie I like with whipped cream,
I just loved it and after I ate it, I had a look on my face because I beam.
Pumpkin pie, I like on Thanksgiving Day,
For my family it was a main part of the meal and was there to stay.
Sweet potato pie was a little harder to cook,
Especially with the recipe used in my family's cookbook.
Cherry pie I loved all the time,
Even though it was a little messy, to not eat it would be a crime.
Banana cream pie was easy to make,
The hardest part was the crust that I had to bake.
Blueberry pie was good but it makes your tongue blue,
It was funny to see your tongue that hue.
Chocolate cream pie I like served cold on a dish,
I loved chocolate so much I wish I could have it all the time…OH I WISH!
Diabetes prohibits my sugar intake or I could die,
Now I am restricted from having my beloved pie.

## Poem #45: The Extracurricular Activities I Did When I Was a Kid

Oh, the extracurricular activities I did when I was just a kid,

All the adventures, athletics, and useful things I did.

Football, I used to be on the offensive line,

I was big and strong, even though I wanted to play other positions, I did not whine.

In soccer, I was getting goals and won,

A lot of games, but more importantly I had fun.

Baseball, I practiced all the time,

But since my dad was not a coach, I didn't play in games that much, it was a crime.

Basketball was an enduring sport,

I used to be good on defense; I was all over the court.

Swimming, I used to be very good in the pool,

I won a lot of ribbons, I thought that was really cool.

I spent a lot of time weightlifting and becoming strong,

It benefited me at other sports where being strong was never wrong.

I used to get a lot of awards and honors at 4-H, for I did a lot of work,

I overheard other kids and parents who thought, because of all my accolades, I was a jerk.

Boy Scouts, I did a lot, like camping and a lot of hikes,

I was doing important moral things to grow up when I was a tyke.

I used to help other kids and tutor them to lessen their strife,

With academics so they could learn something for the rest of their life.

I used to mentor other kids, as a peer,

Most of the time it helps others just to lend an ear.

Volunteering in my community, I did what was right,

To save the streets from trash and help animal shelters from their plight.

All of those memories I would not get rid,

For they molded me into a prosperous adult, from being a good kid.

# Poem #46: Pets I Had Growing Up

There were many pets I had growing up with my family,
We raised them with love and they were important to me.
Dachshunds we had outside until it was cold,
Then we brought them inside so they could grow old.
A German Shepard we had for a little time,
It tore up our garage and it looked like a scene of a crime.
We had many cats and they used to hunt mice at our home,
They also hunted other animals if, into our yard, they would roam.
Chickens we had and they laid plenty of eggs,
They ran around their roost on their little chicken legs.
Since we had a pond, we had plenty a duck,
To see them waddle around and feed them bread, they were in luck.
When migrating, our pond attracted many geese,
They were safe to land and have babies in peace.
For cows we had steers and never a bull,
Because bulls were too way aggressive, and with other pets, our yard would be too full.
Goats ate poison ivy and were tame,
I thought the goats were awesome and not lame.
Fish, we hand in their little tank,
They were easy and cheap to take care of, they didn't "break the bank.
We caught a pet turtle fishing in our pond on the hook,
We kept him awhile and then let him go by a brook.
We had pet birds outside the home, out back,
They were many different colors, including black.
For fun we had a pet rock who likes to "play dead",
I got this idea for this pet from TV, and it never shed.
I hope it is plain to see,
I had many pets when I was young growing up with my family.

# Poem #47: Special Words My Family Used

There are words with special meanings to me and my family,
Here are a few words so you can see.
"Possibly" is a definite no,
That idea or statement just has got to go.
"Probably" is a yes even though it doesn't sound,
Positive, just keep reiterating the point or hound.
"Huh?" is a question if a point you make is unclear,
It may have just been a garbled statement or the other person did not hear.
"Whatever" is a word that you concede a point,
Even if the other person's statement was clearly biased and disjoint.
When referring to a person jokingly you say "nerd",
It is not diminishing a person…You Heard?
"Hippie" was when you referenced to a person who was problematic and a pain,
They were problematically stupid and around that person stupidity did reign.
"Cool" was when an idea was accepted by the group,
Everybody liked what you said, the whole troop.
"Ya' know" was a question that was asked to see if you understand,
It was usually asked when a statement was poorly worded, "as thick as sand".
"Howdy" was a friendly way to say "Hi",
It was from our Northern Virginia environment and used it on either a girl or guy.
"Ga'Narley" was used for something disgustingly bad,
It was for something done so disgusting why it was done would make you mad.
"Kathy" was used to address my mom when she was being difficult,
Sometimes she would work your last nerve so calling her "Kathy" was not your fault.
"Aah!" was an expression to show surprise in a negative way,
It was a bad surprise, caught you of guard, and you did not know what to say.
These words had other meanings then in the dictionary to me,
They are words we used colloquially in my family.

## Poem #48: Ode to My Blue Truck

I miss my blue truck every day,
It was used when I bought it for $13,000 dollars I only had to pay.
My favorite thing about the truck was the metal storage cabinet in the back,
I could keep all the stuff for the truck in it, to keep the truck running on track.
The truck was roomy and fit me well,
So my pride for the truck and ego did swell.
I loved how the truck made me feel,
Sitting high and driving through the surroundings made me feel surreal.
The truck also had a decent-sized bed,
Where I could lay in the back and rest my head.
The color was a perfect navy blue,
It was just right for a hue.
I used to go for rides and ride along,
With the radio on singing a song.
Everything in the truck was pristine and not broken,
I loved that truck, for me it was a token,
Of my independence and living free,
And a place for me to be me.
I searched for it on the internet and I found,
The perfect truck that fit me all-around.
When I had to sell it, boy…I did weep,
For I loved that truck really deep.
At night, I hope and pray,
That I can find another perfect truck…I ask God every day.

## Poem #49: Candy Bars Galore

Oh how I used to eat candy bars galore,
Here are some I especially adore.
My all time favorite was Pay Day,
With peanuts all over it, in my diet they were a mainstay.
When I want some chocolate with peanuts, I went for a Baby Ruth,
I like that added chocolate to tell you the truth.
Kit Kats, I especially like the white chocolate with that crunch,
I loved getting them at Halloween…I loved it a bunch.
Reeses Cups with peanut butter I loved cold,
Eating them this way was a not-so-secret secret, I was told.
Heath Bars, with that toffee, I like to eat,
Especially at the movies, where my diet I would cheat.
Snickers, with all its components, would be good apart,
But better together…assembling them was smart.
Milky Way and that caramel was nice and gooey,
It took awhile to eat because it was so chewy.
3 Musketeers had a nougat filling for this food,
They were simple and to want one, I was always in the mood.
Crunch Bar had a crunch with the crispy rice,
Along with the chocolate this candy bar did entice.
Chunk Bar, with peanuts and raisins, I liked to the max,
I used to eat these when I watched TV and tried to relax.
Mr. Goodbar, made of chocolate and peanuts, was a good snack,
It used to be more popular, they should bring it back.
Mounds with the coconut, I loved the taste,
I would eat the whole candy bar and left nothing to waste.
Due to diabetes, candy bars I cannot have anymore,
Even when I see them all over the place, flavors galore.

## Poem #50: Ode to My Adidas Sambas

My favorite shoes, Adidas Sambas, were sent to me by my family,
Even in an inpatient hospital, they lasted until year three.
They were black and not blue,
And perfect for use in a hospital too.
Another person who wore Sambas was a staff named Kurt,
When I first met him we also wore the same type of shirt.
The Sambas size 14 covered my feet well,
It was protective, like an unbreakable shell.
With these sambas, my foot never got wet,
That was good in a hospital setting, as you can bet.
Everyday different chemical and fluids put those shoes to the test,
Those shoes never under-performed…They were the best!
At the hospital, I wore those shoes all day every day,
They were worth the eighty dollars my family had to pay.
Those shoes were way above par,
Especially since I walked an hour and a half each morning…these shoes went far.
The hospital environment, out those shoes went through a lot of strife,
But they held up to the abuse, all of their usable life.
I wore them all the time except when I was asleep,
When they wore out and I had to throw them away, I did weep.
For those were the best shoes that ever belonged to me,
Thank God, they were a gift from my family.

## Poem #51: Ode to Diabetes

Because of Diabetes I have to watch what I eat,
Due to the sugar, I cannot have many a treat.
Every day I have to do a fingerstick,
To monitor my blood sugar, my fingers I have to prick.
I have to watch what I eat for food,
Even if I want sugar, I have to be smart and not give in to my mood.
My biggest meal now is a sensible lunch,
Throughout the day I have to be careful what I munch.
I even have to watch my weight,
So I try not to eat anything late.
I have to eat things like green beans instead,
That lowers my blood sugar, so I won't end up dead.
For exercise I go for a walk or run,
So I can burn off the sugar and be a healthy person.
I even have to watch cereal hot or cold,
Because of the sugar content, truth be told.
I cannot eat concentrated sugar even for a snack,
To make sure my blood sugar doesn't go out of whack.
Diabetes adds a lot of strife,
To my already hectic and busy life.
Diabetes and taking care of it is a marathon and not a race,
I have to watch myself and keep a constant pace,
With diabetes I have to have a lot of self-control and not cheat,
And constantly watch what and how much I have to eat.

# Poem #52: My Daily Schedule I Write Every Day

Every day, I write my schedule on "sticky notes" for the day,
So I can get everything done and have time to play.
My "sticky notes" don't take up too much space,
But they make sure I don't miss an appointment and that I am at the right place.
I can remember my schedule when I write,
My daily schedule down, so I do all my important things right.
Having my schedule in front of me doesn't impair,
Getting things done, without my schedules my life would be a nightmare.
Depending on the day, my schedule can be quite long,
That is why my schedule is in my pocket and I bring it along.
I also put on my "sticky notes" the day's date,
So I have the right day and appointments, so I won't be late.
This scheduling method is perfect for keeping me on time,
Without them I would carelessly miss appointments with no reason or rhyme.
It helps me to remember daily schedules if I can see,
What appointments are associated with me.
The hardest part of the "sticky note" is where to start,
I write my appointments from my calendar, which I think is smart.
Some days a week are slow and the schedules look small all the same,
Usually there is nothing to do…these days are quite boring and lame.
My schedules and routines lessen the strife,
That is associated with my busy life.
"Sticky notes" with my daily schedule are here to stay,
I am accustomed to them and write them in the morning for the day.

## Poem #53: Ode to Lifting Weight

Oh how I love to lift weight,
When I do it I feel great.
Dumbbells, I do things like bicep curl,
A good way to get my biceps to unfurl.
Bench press, I like to go to the max,
And build my chest through the muscles I tax.
Calf raises, I lift my calves to raise.
People see my big calves, and they get jealous and gaze.
Leg press, my big legs lift hard and are a token,
Of hard work that can only be done through effort and not words spoken.
Leg extensions, I could do all night,
In a sitting position, raising you legs, until your legs get tired and you have to push through and give a good "fight".
Leg curls, I do after leg extensions, which is smart,
To try and build all of your legs where each machine does its part.
Squats, I used to do a lot and would feel the "crunch",
That helped me at football, on the offensive line, a whole bunch.
Tricep exercises got my triceps big like my chest,
It helped me do things like pull-ups the best.
Lifting weights has a mindset and attitude,
To make me one big and powerful dude.
I used to lift weight from early to late,
Just my determination, and a whole lot of repetitions and weight.

## Poem #54: Ode to the Beach

Oh how my family and I loved to go to the beach
It was a couple of hours away, easily within a car's reach.
I used to go play in the sand,
And make sand castles and sculptures with a pail in hand.
I used to go and collect many a shell,
The ones that were symmetrically perfect are better, my parents did tell.
Sometimes we had cooked things like hotdogs and hamburger meat,
All the food we bought with us we would eat.
Crabs, we saw and we would give them a name,
Usually named after friends and not something lame.
Birds, we saw would "bug" us and fly,
While we were enjoying ourselves and trying to shew them away, pointlessly...why try!
One time we saw dolphins in the sea,
They were playful and beautiful, between you and me.
I used to go swimming in the water so blue,
I would do simple strokes I know were tried and true.
I would also bring music along,
So when I heard music I liked to sing along with the song.
I would love to lay down in the sun and get a tan,
I liked tanned people, I am definitely a fan.
However, I learned to put sunscreen on my head,
Or at the end of the day it would be burned and red.
All the things I learned at the beach I would teach,
To my little brothers so they too could love the beach.

## Poem #55: Things I Liked in Puerto Rico

I liked when I went to Puerto Rico on a family vacation trip,
We went there by airplane and not by ship.
The "coqui" frogs made a very distinct sound,
That is how we knew they were around us, all-around.
Potato balls full of seasoned meat,
Were my favorite things to eat at the beach while we "beat the heat".
Paella, I had in San Juan, was my favorite meal with seafood,
It is still my favorite seafood meal to do this day, and to eat it, I am always in the mood.
At the south of the island, the Phosphorescent Bay, lit up at night,
Thanks to the moon, the bay was full of light.
In El Yunque, I saw the Las Minas waterfall,
It was at the end of a small hike and was tall.
Sabana Grande was a religious space,
Where the faithful saw the Virgin Mary at this place.
The parrots, I found out the ugly ones talked,
I actually saw some while we were walked in the forest.
I went to see my dad's family,
In the town of Yauco, where they are known for their coffee.
Old San Juan had colorful houses everywhere,
Equally colorful, personality-wise, were the people and their nationalistic/patriotic flare.
El Morro is an old Spanish fort that my family and I spent all day,
Hearing how the old Spanish soldiers sunk other country's ships who got too close and did not stay away.
The Bacardi Rum Plant was pristine and clean,
Its ground were perfect, to say otherwise would be untrue and mean.
A fresh coconut I knocked down from a tree,
It was a great-tasting coconut, believe me.
If you are going to Puerto Rico, here is a tip,
Bring a Spanish-speaking native, like my dad, to enhance your trip.

# Poem #56: T-Rex Versus Triceratops in an Epic Fight

On TV I saw T-Rex and Triceratops get in an epic fight,
Triceratops had to hold his ground while T-Rex tried to get in a bite.
T-Rex wanted to get some fresh meat,
But had to contend with Triceratops' three horns in order to eat.
Besides Triceratops had the advantage of being lower to the ground,
So T-Rex tried to flank him by going around,
Triceratops' horns so he could prey,
But Triceratops kept up his guard and his actions told T-Rex, "\Not today!".
The T-Rex had a cumbersome frame,
To try and lunge at Triceratops in this lethal game.
T-Rex wanted Triceratops for lunch,
But Triceratops tried to gourd T-Rex with his horns, which, if successful, would hurt a bunch.
T-Rex was trying to have Triceratops for a snack,
And to save itself, Triceratops wanted to put T-Rex on the ground and on his back.
Triceratops made a great stand,
To defend himself and protect his land.
But T-Rex made eating Triceratops his quest,
And both of them fought their best.
T-Rex saw Triceratops as food,
But Triceratops wasn't going down easy, it had attitude.
Since Triceratops was my favorite dinosaur, it is easy to see,
Why I watched that epic battle on TV.
I can tell you the fight scene was not long,
But I was enthralled and followed along.
Both dinosaurs fought with all of their might,
To eat or not be eaten was the motivation of this fight.

## Poem #57: Ode to Erectile Dysfunction (ED)

Having Erectile Dysfunction (ED) really does suck,

Even if a woman is willing, you are out of luck!

It is caused by my mental health medication,

I saw on a legal website that my psychiatric medications and ED have a direct correlation.

So now my penis doesn't work,

And if I go on a date and a woman is in the mood, I get to be the jerk,

And say that my "manhood" is broken,

There are no other words that need to be spoken.

If a woman finds out, then with her friends she will jest,

Because as a guy you are "disqualified", even if, on a date, I tried my best.

I used to take an ED pill,

Due to my insurance won't pay for it, I had to stop this medication, because, to the insurance company, ED is not an ill.

I wish the insurance people would do what is right,

And help me "intrigue" a woman at night.

But no, so it is just a crying shame,

That when it comes to sexual activity, I am lame.

I just wish I could get erect and have a moment of "release",

So I can attract a woman and be at peace.

With ED I feel like less of a guy,

And with no way to afford ED pills, then why try!

I would just love to go on a date,

And impress a woman to want to stay late,

But without being able to get erect, affects my attitude,

And as a guy with ED trying to impress a woman, I am not in the mood.

Lord knows, to get erect I would need a truck,

Load of ED pills, so my love life would not suck.

## Poem #58: Ode to My Worst Boss

My masters advisor was my worst boss to date,
Due to all the stress I was under, I gained a lot of weight.
He did not know how to lead people…NO WAY!
So I did not get my PhD there at the University or Virginia, also known as UVA.
He did not know how to use his head,
He would "bad mouth" me to his colleagues instead.
Nastier, around me he used to pass a lot of gas,
Even though I told him many times to stop, he did it to harass.
He would not tell you what to do and about you he would jest,
And complain I wasn't doing enough, ever though I was doing my very best.
Every suggestion I had was a "no go",
But two weeks later he would propose the same idea, like I would not know!
He would always yell at me and gave me attitude,
And the comments he said to me where really crude.
A lot of times he would "piss me off" so much I would just go to lunch,
I left because I was so mad at him; I almost gave him a punch.
I knew if I wanted to get something done it was up to me,
So I just did all my ideas and work "behind his back" and just "let it be".
Due to his stupidity, it took my masters degree extra time,
And it cost me my PhD, which to me was a crime.
With my masters advisor it was always a game,
Where he got so "nasty" against me, it was a shame.
He may have had a PhD but was no manager,
And he could always "bad mouth" me to others, which professionally put me in danger.
I can tell you no truer words were spoken,
When I "told him off" and said my trust in him was broken.
The promises of great opportunity was his bait,
But for me, my masters advisor was the biggest jerk I had for a boss to date.

## Poem #59: Types of Food That Delight Me

For me, there are many food that I delight,
Here are some that fit me just right.
Puerto Rican food, like mofongos and pasteles, are awfully good,
Would I go to a Puerto Rican restaurant? Yes I would!
Enchiladas and tacos are Mexican foods I like,
I have been eating them since I was a little tyke.
English foods are tasty like chips and fish,
I wish I had a plate of that right now…Oh I Wish!
American Southern food classics have a good spice,
I like it so much and have so much I have a full stomach, that's nice.
New England foods I like include clam chowder soup,
I have made it before for my whole troop.
Texas ribs and brisket are foods that are cooked a certain way,
To get their particular flavor I would like to eat every day.
German food like schnitzel and spaetzle are favorites of mine,
Eating them every day would be just fine.
French food including chicken cordon bleu is made of ham chicken and cheese,
I like French food and would I have it again? Yes please!
Italian eggplant and chicken parmesan are good with garlic bread,
I eat so much of it I "pass out" in my bed.
Mediterranean food with yellow rice and spiced meat,
Is very delightful and something I like to eat.
Chinese food like beef and broccoli I won't waste,
It has a unique flavor, I like the taste.
Japanese food especially shrimp teriyaki I always had for lunch,
It had a wonderful flavor with a prestigious punch.
These foods were wonderful and I won't fight,
The urge to eat these foods and my subsequent feelings of delight.

# Poem #60: Just Another Patient

At Whiting Forensic Hospital (WFH), I am just another patient, which is just a disservice to me,
The staff at WFH treats me like that because I am under the Psychiatric Security and Review Board, the PSRB.
From my academic record, the staff can see I have a masters degree and I am smart,
But the WFH staff doesn't care because they have no heart.
My behavior at the hospital was the best,
Even when staff abused me physically and verbally, just to test,
My resolve and try to hold me at WFH, and do extra punitive time,
Even though I was found not guilty by reason of mental defect for a crime.
The staff did their best to try and make me lose my cool,
To up my medication, which staff did to many lower-functioning patients to try and make them "act a fool".
I even kept my hygiene impeccable and every day I bathed,
And every time we were allowed to, I went and shaved.
I even watched my blood sugar with special meals, including lunch,
I even watched what I had for snacks to munch.
However, to WFH staff, that did not matter or care,
All they wanted was to try and antagonize me and "get in my hair".
The staff did their best to make my life hard,
And had no trouble treating you like a "retard".
They would try to attack me, with a patient's weakness, as bait,
To try to "piss off" me off, to try and get me irate,
The staff did it to try and get extra pay,
By trying to put me on constant observation (CO), to do overtime watching a patient that they had "pissed off" by their actions that day.
For the staff, "pissing off" patients was fun,
Heaven forbid somebody did that to their daughter or son.
For staff to rile up a patient is just a game,
And the patient had to pay the price, which is a shame!
I am glad the news covered staff victimizing a patient and put that on TV,
For abusing patients, but many more patients were abused, including me.

## Poem #61: Ode to Being a Research Scientist

Being a research scientist is the best,
Here are some of my adventures and fulfilling them was my quest.
Novel Energetics, I developed "skins" for missiles that fly,
And "take out"other missiles like a "grenade rocket" so nobody on our side will die.
Thermobarics, I developed materials that would be used against a cave,
Full of enemy combat units, think how many of our soldiers these materials could save.
Alane or Aluminum Trihydride I made for solid rocket fuel,
Making that with a reactor full of pressurized hydrogen at a specific temperature was cool.
Memristors, I used Titanium Oxide to make a resistor that could have memory and "think",
And kept a computer on applications when it was turned off, so users would not make a stink.
I developed sol-gels for oxide engine materials and gemstones to boot,
I could create different colors with different oxides, what a hoot!
For non-oxide composites, I made a silicon carbide polymer for a jet engine with a punch,
And it was well sought after, multiple companies wanted it a bunch.
Chemical Vapor Deposition (CVD), I developed conditions for many a non-oxide and oxide coat,
I still have these conditions because in notebooks, I wrote.
I used laser ablation for nanoscale drug delivery coatings for my masters degree,
I set-up the whole lab and did the research, I was very proud of me.
I cooked carbon microspheres with Aluminum CVD precursors for a missile storage cabinet wall,
Just in case a bomb hits a ship's ammo dump, the ship won't fall.
Type II-VI semiconductors could vary the cations for different wavelength illumination,
I made thin films of these materials with pulsed laser ablation.
I made Platinum nanoparticles and nanoparticles with many other metals,
For many uses like making synthetic leaves and flower petals.
I made, via CVD, silicon-coated iron powder for a magnetic particle with radiation shield,
To protect our nation's aircraft, who had parts made from this powder to wield.
Every one of these projects and more put me to the test,
But each one made me, as a scientist, good, better, and the best.

## Poem #62: Having a Pond at My Family's House

It was great to have a pond at our house and has special memories for me,
It was man-made, built by my family.
We had stocked our pond with fish,
So we could catch them, clean them and cook them for our dinners. Delish!
It was great to see the setting sun,
On our pond, when the day was done.
Migrating birds landed at our pond like geese,
To rest and some had families, in peace.
We also had many a duck,
They would waddle and swim around, and we watched them. What luck!
We would put, in the pond, a remote-controlled boat,
And it would whip around, bob, and float.
The potato launcher we used to hit a floating target in our pond,
The memories of working with my brothers on this, I am fond.
We found crayfish in our pond and used them as bait,
To catch fish and they were good to use and that was great!
My family used our pond to let our pet animals drink,
It was good for keeping our pet animals hydrated, for them it was a common link.
If it was cold enough in the winter we would walk on the ice,
But I was nervous not to fall through, that would not be nice.
We caught, in our pond, a pet turtle with a hook,
We let it go miles away, beside a brook.
We used to toss our dogs in the shallows for a swim,
They doggy-paddled their tails off, both her and him.
When we dug out our pond, we found bullets from the American Civil War,
We kept them on the mantle in the family room, next to the closet door.
It was a lot of fun to have a pond as you can see,
At our house to be enjoyed by my family and me.

## Poem #63: Ice Cream Flavors Galore

Throughout my life, I have eaten ice cream flavors galore,

Here are some of the ice cream flavors I adore.

Cookie and cream depends on the type of cookie,

I like Oreos because I am a veteran of eating this flavor and not a rookie.

Butter pecan is so creamy and nutty with a distinct flavor,

It is my dad's favorite and it is an ice cream flavor I savor.

Caramel ice cream has a caramel swirl which is good,

Would I put more caramel in it? Yes I would!

Vanilla is good alone or in a milkshake,

When I am given vanilla, I get more than my fair take.

Chocolate is good especially when it is creamy and smooth,

It has a very satisfying taste that for me will soothe.

Strawberry is a flavor I liked later in life,

It tastes so darn good it melts away my strife.

Mint chocolate chip has really good chocolate chunks in mint,

Especially if it has Andes chocolate chunks, any ice cream companies getting a hint?

Cinnamon ice cream was used in an ice cream that tasted like an oatmeal pie,

That was one awesome ice cream I was glad to have before I die.

Cherry ice cream has nice big pieces of cherry fruit,

I wasn't sure if I would like it but now this flavor has a new recruit.

Maple Walnut tastes like maple syrup and is nutty,

I like eating this ice cream alone or with a buddy.

Key lime ice cream I like but I have to warn is tart,

But I like its "flavorable attitude" and it is a flavor near and dear to my heart.

Rocky Road is a mix of flavors that I eat when I relax,

Together the flavors are wonderful and push the "final outcome" flavor to the max.

If I didn't have diabetes, the ice cream flavors I would have more,

For there are many ice cream flavors, ice cream flavors galore.

# Poem #64: Ode to Stairs

Throughout my life I have gone up and down many a flight of stair,

I have to climb them up and down to get in and out of my apartment lair.

Going up and down flights of stairs changes your attitude,

Each stair just bugs the heck out of me and makes me more rude.

I have to climb the stairs just to eat,

And to go to my bedroom again I have to climb down full of vegetables and meat.

I wish I had a one-floor house so I can live in peace,

From going up and down stairs, so much tension would release.

It just adds unneeded strife,

To climb stairs all of my life.

To go anywhere I have to climb stairs day and night,

I just have to ask, does that seem right?

Everyday climbing the stairs, more of the same,

For those who cannot walk, their stuck, what a crying shame!

Heaven forbid you tumble and fall,

If I fell, I would fall down the stairs and into a wall.

I wish I had extra money and space,

To put in a trusty elevator, to eliminate stairs, in my place.

Every day I have to "brave" the stairs and start,

Getting ready for the day, with stairs, making my muscles hurt and smart.

When I climb the stairs I feel my knees crunch,

And believe me that hurts, hurts a whole bunch.

All the words, in this poem, I have spoken,

At least I am in fairly good shape with no leg bones broken.

If I had broken leg bones, then I would be dead,

Because I could not climb the stairs and be almost confined to my bed.

Always climbing stairs will make me rip out my hair,

All because of the incessant climbing of all the flights of stair.

## Poem #65: My Poem, Only Time Will Tell

To get into a college summer camp, I wrote a poem titled, "Only Time Will Tell",
It was so great and mesmerizing, I was under its spell.
Just like this poem, the lines did rhyme,
To do this, finding the right words took a lot of time.
I was saying and writing verses all day,
It felt very fulfilling in a creative way.
My brothers did chime in and sang along,
Until my poem got too long.
I was working on it until late,
Even though it was months before the due date.
I was just "feeling it" and in the mood,
I just felt like being a very creative and imaginative literary dude.
The verse just kept filling my head,
I had to get them on paper before I lost them. Oh dread!
I just kept writing and sitting in my chair,
And worked until I wrote everything I wanted because I care,
To finish this work on paper,
So I could go to this college summer camp, which was my caper.
How I carefully crafted this poem was a token,
Of how thoughtful I was writing and no verses were broken.
I wrote this poem pure and from the heart,
And I can tell you this poem got me into that summer camp, it did its part.
That is why I remember, to this day, the poem's name,
And I wish I had published it. What a shame!
For this poem I thought was my best,
Especially when I got into camp, which was the poem's quest.
Even though the poems I write now are swell,
There will only be one poem named, "Only Time Will Tell".

## Poem #66: Favorite Channels on TV

How I love the programs on my favorite channels on TV,
I like many different channels with different unique things to see.
ESPN has many different sports on day and night,
They even show the best of past sports like a really good boxing fight.
TNT, like ESPN, has games of basketball,
You can watch all night and see players with names big and small.
FX and FXX has movies that are good,
Do I prefer watching movies on these channels? Yes, I would!
SYFY, I like the fantasy movies that make me think,
They play good movies on this channel that don't stink.
The Comedy Channel plays Southpark and other funny programs that are great,
When I was younger I watched these programs and stayed up way too late.
Food Network makes good food and is kind of a tease,
Because if I could makes food of that quality, I would say yes please!
TLC, I like to watch Dr. Pimplepopper alone,
Because some of the work she does is nasty and makes me groan.
Much Music, I get to hear music from over the years,
I get to hear those songs again with my own ears.
Nickelodeon, I get to watch SpongeBob and other cartoons,
 They are funny and quick-witted, what a bunch of maroons!
Disney Channel, I watched when I was a kid,
I like when they put together music videos with the oldies. Yes I did!
MTV, I liked music videos a bunch,
I used to watch them and snack on something to munch.
History Channel, I like documentaries about war,
They did their best to keep it interesting, not a bore.
Those are some of my favorite channels from me,
Thank goodness for TV channels! What did people do before TV?

## Poem #67: Books That Influenced Me

Throughout my life I have been influenced by many a book,

These stories were so intriguing to me; they dug in their distinctive hook.

*Picture of Dorian Grey* was about a man who never aged or seemed weathered when he did something wrong.

His picture did and if he hadn't looked at his picture he would have lived long.

*Brave New World* talked about a person being developed and born in a specific class,

No matter how hard tried you stayed in that class and never more would a person amass.

*The Prince* was about power politics and what a leader should know,

It had examples of leaders and action, like in war when to initiate and go.

*Atlas Shrugged* was about when all the "brains" took a break,

The country stalled until the "brains" came back and the country would "wake".

*Undying Glory* was about the first colored regiment of the American Civil War,

With a big part when that unit attacked a southern confederate fort by a sea shore.

*Animal Farm* used animals to depict people and symbols and was a work of art,

It showed how communism actually worked and how different peoples/animals did their part.

*Heart of Darkness* had a lot of imagery and detail,

But I wanted more action, and excessive detail I would curtail.

*Beowulf* showed the life and code of ancient old,

Times where stories were not written but many were told.

*The Jungle* talked about people and industry of the time, like food,

I did not eat sausage for five years due to the book's description of how it was made. It was truly crude!

*The Metamorphosis* was about a man who turned into a bug,

Not even his family wanted him, he could not get a hug.

*The Time Machine* went to the future in time,

How one race of humans ate the other was a natural crime.

*The Invisible Man* the main character had a hard life,

Because he was invisible and caused himself and a lot of people strife.

For these stories, I went to the library and took a look,

And found these influential stories and their respective book.

## Poem #68: Ode to Baked Beans

Baked beans are a food I like to eat,
With many different flavors, I can eat them until I am replete.
From a TV show, I found that baked beans are made from Navy beans that are white.
After cooking, they change colors and taste for a more "colorful" bite.
After talking to a chef, baked beans take many hours to cook,
But the taste is fantastic and worth all the time that it took.
I had baked beans in a restaurant from a crock,
They were fantastic, fresh like that. Those baked beans rock!
I have had baked beans as an entrée or a side dish,
Every time I wanted more, oh I wish!
Original flavor is plain and good,
I would eat more of these beans, yes I would.
Barbeque flavor is great with that saucy tang,
At my house, my family ate them and they were gone in a bang.
Molasses flavor makes the baked beans sweet,
I like them even more if you add Siracha for some heat.
Maple Hickory are cooked for a distinct taste,
I eat them all and not let a bean go to waste.
Brown sugar and bacon flavor is sweet with some salt,
If I have to choose between flavors, this is my default.
Bacon, alone, with baked beans are good for lunch,
The bacon gives those beans a meaty punch.
Onion flavor makes the baked beans good for a snack,
The oniony sweet flavor keeps my tastebuds on track.
Vegetarian baked beans I now try,
Because they are better for my diabetes, so I won't die.
Baked beans are good as a wholesome treat,
And they are better for you than a lot of other foods you can eat.

## Poem #69: My Favorite Classes in School

I like to pay homage to my favorite classes in school,
In these classes, I learned many a professional tool.
Chemistry, I learned how to do many a reaction large and small,
From the beginning, I learned of my materials science call.
Physics, I learned the forces of motion,
For big interstellar bodies to the waves of the ocean.
Biology, I learned that animals minimize energy and are inherently lazy.
To waste energy on frivolous things, in nature, is just plain crazy.
In Calculus, I learned the rate of change and the area under a curve,
From derivatives and integrals, respectively, that helped me in making grades, in a positive swerve.
Computer Science, I learned to program in Pascal, Ada, and HTML for the internet,
These languages are why I am good at computers, I bet.
World History, I learned about things of the human past,
"Those who do not learn from history are doomed to repeat it", has never been truer, not while world problems last.
Unites States History, I learned a lot about war,
My class covered all American conflicts, and how that opened the American diplomatic door.
United States Politics, I learned that it is easy to "ride on another's coattails",
Rather than do something new that your opponent can derail.
Scanning Electron Microscopy class helped me learn how to use this microscope,
When it comes to imaging, I can get great focus, I have "hope".
Geography of Sub-Saharan Africa, I learned that Africa has a lot of natural resources,
But almost every other continent steals from them as a matter of discourses.
Spanish, I took to level five,
But I barely know enough now to keep me alive.
Nuclear Physics, I learned about atoms and how they work,
In Advanced Nuclear Physics, I used perturbation theory to see many a atom's quirk.
I learned from my favorite classes so I won't be a fool,
Because I my knowledge is well-rounded after going to school.

## Poem #70: Crushes of My Life

I have had many crushes on women throughout my life,
I even almost made one of my crushes my wife.
Lara, she was the crush I almost married but I had to let her go,
I have reminisced and pondered whether I did the right think, more than you know.
Teresa, she was a red-head and very smart,
She was awfully nice to me and had a big heart.
Beth, she was athletic, good at sports, and popular with many a guy,
She had so many guys interested in her I said, "Why try?".
Julie was blond with blue eyes and really cute,
I tried to talk to her but around her I was mute.
Heather, when she was younger, I asked her on a date,
But when she grew older, I wasn't interested because she put on too much weight.
Karen, let's face it she had a big well-developed chest,
But she was also in my physics classes and we competed to see who was the best.
Melissa, she was in my Spanish class and for a project, I went to her home,
I spent hours getting ready, even did my hair with hairspray and a comb.
Aimee, she was in great shape because she liked to run,
But by the time I asked her out, she was already with someone.
Michelle,, she was adorable but she like to cut,
After spending time with her, I found out she was crazy, a complete nut.
Katie, she was so beautiful that I could just stare,
But she talked all about my foibles. So I did not ask her out,. I did not dare!
Sara, she was my first crush and I, in library class in first grade, gave her a kiss,
She was a wonderful person; her mental warmness was what I miss.
Lauren, she was a girl that I used to go to lunch,
All the time, I was infatuated with her a bunch.
I never got too serious with any of these crushes, which caused me strife,
But oh well, got to keep going, such is life.

## Poem #71: Ode to Fishing

In our family's pond I liked to fish all day,
And either clean and eat the fish or let them go, in the water, away.
How I let the line cast,
And leave all my problems in the past.
How I knew the different parts of the pond,
The deeper section by the overflow pipe where the big fish were fond.
How I went to relax when I had an attitude,
To just go fish and maybe catch some food.
How the fish on the line put up a fight,
When the fish went after my earthworm bait in one bite.
How I used to clean the fish with their characteristic crunch,
When you took the head off to cook them for lunch.
How I used to dig for the earthworm bait,
To try and catch bigger fish with more weight.
How I used to bring my tacklebox along,
Just in case, I needed something like other baits and lures when earthworms were wrong.
How I used to fish as if it were a quest,
To try and catch the biggest fish that tasted the best.
How I used to try and catch the most fish as if it were a game,
And try to keep a few of the big ones, all the same.
How I had to fix the line if the line was broken,
And the fish kept the hook, as if it were a token.
How I used to go back up to my home,
With a bucket full of big fish, which were heavy up the hill I had to roam.
How I loved the catfish to eat,
They were easy to clean and had a lot of meat.
Fishing was a real relaxing way,
To enjoy the summer with a mini-fishing trip that took all day.

## Poem #72: My Favorite X-Men

X-Men was my favorite superhero team to me,
I used to read them in comic books and watch them on TV.
Colossus was my favorite with muscles and skin of metal to pound,
Bad guys hard enough to put them in the ground.
Cyclops was the leader and had an optical eye blast,
That dismantled bad guys and put them in a cast.
Wolverine had claws and could heal quick in a fight,
He had the attitude and abilities to fight all day and night.
Storm could manipulate weather and fly,
She could hit a bad guy with a lightning storm and watch him or her fry.
Rogue had the ability to get powers she would "steal",
But she couldn't touch anyone, so alone she must feel.
Kitty Pride had the power to walk through a wall,
She could take down a bad guy no matter how big or tall.
Professor X was the team's "brain",
But he was confined to a wheelchair, not even a cane.
Beast was muscular and had fur that was blue,
He was very dexterous and could fight, true!
Iceman could freeze things with the power of ice,
Wouldn't it hurt to be frozen solid, that wouldn't feel nice.
Jubilee could emit energy from her hands,
She could take out enemies were ever here energy lands.
Nightcrawler was a very good fighter and could teleport in his quest,
To complete the mission and be at his best.
Jean Grey was extremely powerful but humble,
Because she did not want to bring out the Dark Phoenix, who was always ready to rumble.
It wasn't only that I liked the X-Men but my whole family,
They had different favorite X-Men than me.

# Poem #73: Ode to Walking

I go for a walk every day,
While I am walking I like to daydream and mentally play.
I like to walk and cover a lot of ground,
I walk everywhere around my house until a god route I have found.
When I walk I feel less tension and free,
I be myself and pay attention to me.
I like to walk to new places near and far,
And it is much healthier than riding in a car.
When I am walking I am friendly and say, "Hi!",
To everybody I cross paths with girl or guy.
When I am walking I like to "get in my own head",
To make sure I am mentally healthy and well instead.
Sometimes I, when I walk, sing a song,
Especially when I am walking a distance that is long.
I like to walk further and further so I dare,
To walk to further and further monuments before I walk back to my apartment lair.
The time to myself during a walk, I crave,
To keep my sanity in my hectic world, for myself I save.
I like to walk and bring out my best,
To do more exercise is my quest.
When I walk, mentally and physically, I have fun,
And regret when my walk is over and done.
I will say, if I have a good walk route, I keep the same,
Route because to get rid of a good walk route is a shame.
When I walk, I see new things and roam,
And reminisce about what I saw on the walk when I get home.
The best thing about a walk is that I don't have to pay,
Because a walk is free and I go for a walk every day.

## Poem #74: Restaurants in Danbury, Connecticut

Here are my favorite restaurants while I am under the stranglehold of the Psychiatric Security and Review Board, the PSRB,
In the Connecticut community I chose to go in Danbury.
Agave had excellent Mexican food with mole sauce,
And all I have to say is that the sauce was boss.
JKs, I like their steak and eggs with scrambled eggs with cheese,
It was only a few minute walk from my house, so would I go? Yes please!
TKs had chicken wings on my birthday I could eat,
I know many a patron who would eat until they were replete.
Planet Pizza had very good pizza by the slice,
They would have the pizza on display, just to entice.
Kibberia had great Mediterranean food and was clean,
The schwarma and falafel, I had, I was very keen.
Puerta Vallarta had good enchiladas and plates full of plenty of food,
To eat there again, I am always in the mood!
Duchess had breakfast sandwiches that were just right,
After a long evening where I had not eaten all night.
Planeta Brazil had meat and side dishes on a buffet,
All that I can say is that I had many a tray.
Soho Pizza had pizza with very good crust,
I go there a lot as you can trust.
Good Taste had Chinese food with plenty of flavor,
I enjoyed their beef and broccoli so much the taste I would savor.
Amigos had Spanish food with a pernil that was so delish,
To this day, I enjoyed that food and the memories I still relish.
Elmers Deli had a ham and cheese omelet that was the best,
I ever had, indeed it passed the test.
These restaurants in Danbury were the best to me,
And made my life livable under the oppressive and tyrannical PSRB.

## Poem #75: Ode to Obscure Holidays

When I worked on my psychosocial club's newsletter, I reported on many an obscure holiday,
There are obscure holidays nearly every day.
There are many national month holidays in my life,
Like national bee month due to September being the month bees are out causing me strife.
There are national obscure holidays because of the news,
They are smaller in recognition and they won't have days off of work but they amuse.
Obscure holidays like the Day of Infamy where people did die,
But I know the history of this obscure holiday because I am a "military history guy".
There are some holidays that will help me pass a math test,
Like Pi day, where they serve pie in jest.
There are some obscure holidays that show I as a person care,
Like Grandparent's Day, with family members I share.
There are smaller obscure holidays where we atone,
Like D-Day Day, where many soldiers died alone.
Then there are holidays that celebrate the foods I eat,
Like baklava, and other foods I eat as a treat.
There are even holidays to celebrate animals like a cat,
Not only the skinny ones, but ones like Garfield who are fat.
There are even holidays for new adventures in space,
Like when America got to the moon and "won" the space race.
There are holidays to be celebrated by the young,
Back in the day, they used to celebrate some of the holidays with a bell being rung.
There are obscure holidays for sports,
Like the championships of smaller and lesser-known games played by their dedicated cohorts.
There are holidays to be celebrated by the old,
With their stories, which are passed by being told.
There are many obscure holidays that will stay,
Because they celebrate things that matter to people like me, our personal obscure holiday.

## Poem #76: Hurry Up and Wait

Don't you hate it in life when people make you hurry up and wait?
Here they force me to rush, rush, rush just to wait for them. Oh Great!
There these people think they're so important they spin you around,
Just to make you have to wait and sit and be let down.
I am used to a lot of appointments doing that to me,
Shackled to their schedules when I want to be free.
Here I get into to trouble if I say a peep,
Getting sheparded around like a sheep.
However you need the appointment so why should I try,
To tell them how I feel waiting and all you can do is sigh.
Since I had to hurry I am not in the mood,
To wait for their convenience so I might give them attitude.
After all the anxiety-provoking hurry to wait is a nightmare,
Then they wonder why I "tear out my hair".
The way they are taking advantage of my time,
Shouldn't they be held accountable for a stealing crime?
They will cover-it-up and make themselves look good on paper,
Even though they inconvenienced me in their caper.
The time and effort I had no choice but gave,
Even though I wanted to tell them how I feel. Oh I crave!
These people who hurry me just to wait are playing a game,
With me being the pawn. How lame!
I would like to tell them how I feel and get it off my chest,
But those people, at the "water cooler", will just jest.
Hurry up and wait, I have done my whole life,
This caused me a lot of internal strife.
If I try to hurry them, they ask if you have a date,
No, I just don't want the aggravation of hurrying up just to wait.

# Poem #77: Movies That Get My Attention

There are certain movies that really entertain me,
When I watch these movies on TV.
*Spaceballs* is about the adventures of a space captain and his "mog",
Who goes up against Dark Helmet and the other bad guys in this comedic fog.
*Blazing Saddles* is a comedy about the old west,
Challenging then in taboo situations to save their town from the railroad expansion is their quest.
*Commando* is a movie where a daughter is saved by a military guy,
The awesome hacienda shootout scene makes you ask, "How many bad guys got shot and in the movie, and had to die?".
*Predator* is about an alien warrior on the hunt,
All the actors were huge and muscle-bound, not any of them were a runt.
*Independence Day* is about earth's response to an alien attack,
Where the main characters figure out how to "take down" the aliens and have the world's back.
*Wreck-it Ralph* is about an arcade bad guy who wants to go good,
In the end he does the right thing, like he should.
*The Greatest Showman* is a musical about P.T. Barnum and his circus show,
He, in the end, learns the power of family and stops being on the go.
*Lion King* is about a son of a king that takes over the pride,
But for awhile he thought he was responsible for something really bad and thought best to hide.
*Megamind* is about a bad guy who is blue,
He ended up being the hero and saving everybody too.
*Robin Hood Men In Tights* is a comedy about Robin Hood and his merry men,
They saved the day by infiltrating the bad guy's den.
*Toy Story* is an animated movie with a lot of heart,
Where the toys accepted and cherished each other, this movie is a work of art.
*Harry Potter* movies are about a magical school,
That helps Harry Potter defeat bad guys with many a magical tool.
These movies help my imagination run free,
And helps me be entertained and relaxed, which is a great service to me.

## Poem #78: Cartoons I Used To Watch

The cartoons I used to watch would still be great today,
Many of them I used to watch after school and on Saturday.
*Eek The Cat* was a cartoon about a purple cat who said, "It Never hurts to help!",
But then he would try and receive many a whelp.
*The Tick* was a blue superhero in this comedic cartoon,
He used to go in to battle with the battle cry, "Spoon!".
*Dragon's Lair* had a knight named Dirk,
Who tried to save the day but looked like a goofy jerk.
*Mask* was about vehicles who had a second vehicle in it, like a boat in a car,
To see the secondary vehicles made this cartoon a star.
*Captain N and the Game Masters* was about a teen with a controller and a light gun,
Who teamed up with old Nintendo game superheroes to enhance the fun.
*GI Joe* was about soldiers who fought terrorists and in the end,
Had a good morale at the end of the episode, more decency in kids to mend.
*Exo Squad* was a cartoon where humans fought Neo Sapiens in space,
It was about a fighting group in assault suits and all were an ace.
*Thundercats* were fighting humanoid cats, which my favorite was blue,
They fought together with unique skills and powers against Mumra too.
*Tazmania* was about Taz and his family,
With his dad dragging on in a conversation, was funny to me.
*Tiny Toons* were kids, who had different and unique attitudes,
Interacting with each other, they were hilarious dudes.
*Animaniacs* were two brothers and a sister, who go along,
Doing funny antics and even did a few funny song.
*Super Mario Brothers* was an after school show about the video game,
On Fridays, they would feature Link from Legend of Zelda. Why didn't they show him more was a shame!
These cartoons let kids' minds imagine and play,
Not like the "educational" cartoons they show today.

# Poem #79: Ode to Grocery Shopping at the Grocery Store

I love grocery shopping at the grocery store,
There is so much to see when you go through the door.
There are so many different foods to try,
I am only limited by myself to how much and what I want to buy.
I used to go shopping for my family,
So what everybody ate depended on me.
I used to get meat "by the pound",
From bacon to sausage to hot dogs to beef that was ground.
As I go through the store, there was many a treat,
So much to savor and delight while I eat.
I used to get foods that were good like chicken breast,
But I also got fresh vegetables, they were the best!
I used to go grocery shopping not only for work but for fun,
I used to get food for planned meals when I was done.
I used to get good fruit like a pear,
Or more unique fruit like kiwi if I dare.
I used to get desserts like a cookie,
When I was an inexperienced shopper, a rookie.
I used to get ready-made food for a snack,
But I got healthy food to get my body back on track.
I used to look at some food and groan,
Because I knew it would be bad for my blood sugar and I would leave it alone.
I used to try and take my time shopping and not race,
Because each thing I wanted was in a different place.
I would shop for awhile and take my time,
Because missing something on my shopping list would be a crime.
When I went shopping I wanted more,
Because I was happiest during the week at the grocery store.

## Poem #80: What I Like About Chips

In my life I ate many a chip,
From potato to corn, I liked them alone, with salsa, or with a specialty chip dip.
Original potato chips were good with a crunch,
I liked to put them in my sandwich for a satisfying lunch.
Ruffles potato chips had ridges that hold a lot of flavor,
I also liked the extra crunch that I savor.
Tortilla chips with salsa I liked to eat,
I liked them also in nachos, they couldn't be beat.
Corn chips had a certain unique flavor to taste,
I enjoyed them a lot and not a one I would let go to waste.
There were other chips made of things like bagels I liked to bite,
With specific flavors these chips taste just right!
Chili and cheese especially with corn chips were good with a mild spice,
I always found them alluring and for me, they would entice.
For ruffle potato chips my favorite were sour cream and cheddar,
For awhile in my life, for chips they didn't get much better.
For original potato chips I liked them flavored with that barbeque tang,
I would eat them through a family-sized bag in a bang.
Also, honey barbeque flavor was awesome and goes without being spoken,
That the honey made them sweet but my blood sugar meter would be broken.
Sour cream and onion was a flavor that I wish,
Could always be eaten with chili in my dinner dish.
Ranch potato chips just blew away the rest,
Because they were my "go to" when I was in a mood that was not the best.
Salt and vinegar flavor was good because the taste would linger,
And I liked the vinegar taste so much I would like it off my finger.
Chips were so good they could make me do a back flip,
That is why I enjoyed eating a good chip.

# Poem #81: Please, I Want A Paper Copy

With everything in electronic versions/copies today,
I want my items in paper; I guess I am old-fashioned in that way.
Oh Please! Oh Please! Just give me a book!
Books on computers hurt my eyes after awhile, so I cannot look.
I rather have the more intimate greeting of a paper card,
Because getting emotions from a text or email is very hard.
I rather have somebody put in the effort for a handwritten note,
I prefer it to something on a computer screen, it gets my vote.
I like when I get a paper message from somebody I love,
Handwritten with personality from my turtledove.
In person with a written note it is easy to be smitten,
But people can misrepresent emotions on a computer or phone, and misunderstand what I have written.
Most people think it is wrong to break up when something has gone wrong,
On a computer, especially in a message that is short and not long.
I think it is more personal to write on paper,
What I want to say, with my personality to any specific caper.
I think it is easier to avoid a fight,
If a letter is handwritten and took effort to write.
It is just that paper copies show I took the personal time,
And not just wrote a mass-email to subjugate everybody, which is a crime.
Just to send an email to everybody, to all of the rest,
Shows that I am not giving somebody personal attention, which, in most situations, is the best.
I prefer people writing in ink that is blue or black,
To show people had personal regard for what they wrote, and keep both people on track.
Plus, how you write something shows your mood,
Irregularities or sloppy writing can show your attitude.
I think they are intangibles that a person will say,
If they write things on paper, I wish people did that more today.

# Poem #82: Bottled Water Versus Tap Water Conundrum

I know people who buy bottled water every day,
To shell out that much money for water, I say, "No Way!".
Even though the water that comes out of the tap,
Is sometimes "off-colored" and tastes like crap.
However, bottled water hurts the environmental fight,
Because of all the excess plastic refuse isn't right.
Some of the water out of the tap looks nasty and crude,
And to pass that as town water, is to their residents, awfully rude!
However bottled water has a danger,
Chemicals that leech out of the plastic, to the body, is a stranger.
But tap water can be easily polluted and fail a safety test,
Showing that tap water quality is not the best.
However, bottled water has minerals added that you drink if you dare,
This could affect different parts of the body, even the drinker's hair.
But tap water has fluoride added so it is not pure,
The specialists say it helps its drinkers, but I am not sure.
However, wildlife can be affected by all the bottled water plastic trash,
But the bottled water companies could care less as long as they get their cash.
But tap water can be contaminated judging by its affect on skin as a person will bathe,
Or some people can see tap water's effects on facial skin when they shave.
However, all the nasty bottle water plastic processing isn't good,
Makes me wonder it their drinkers needs more water bottles or if they need to buy. Bluntly, if they should?
Tap water drains local water resources that people need,
Maybe people who abuse their use of tap water should take heed.
However, bottled water eats gas because it needs to be delivered by truck,
Maybe people who drink bottled water every day should stop the waste of gas and many a buck.
So the bottled water versus tap water conundrum will prey,
On water drinkers, because everybody drinks water just about every day.

## Poem #83: As a Guy Stay Away From Women At Whiting Forensic Hospital (WFH)

At Whiting Forensic Hospital (WFH), stay away from the women if you are a guy,

Because these women are crazy, manipulative, and cause a guy to stay there until he will die.

A guy might think one of the women has a nice butt,

But it is a mental hospital and every woman is nut.

A guy might be attracted to a woman's ample breast,

But trust me it is not worth it not even at their best.

A guy might think a woman has a good face,

But their head may be "up in space".

And if a guy tries to interact the woman could call rape,

The outside charges that come will put the guy in bad shape.

The women at WFH will "work" two guys against each other to get them to fight,

Because the women get their "jollies" out of it, even though it isn't right.

Some of the women will want to have sex,

But with rampant sexually transmitted diseases (STDs) a guy will get a hex.

Plus if something goes wrong WFH will say,

It is all the guy's fault and use it to hold them at WFH and indefinitely elongate his stay.

There are plenty of women who "kiss and tell",

They will get the guy in trouble by "ringing the bell".

Some of the women are so bipolar they will give a guy a different attitude,

By the minute, so you don't know what you are getting, i.e. which mood.

Heaven forbid, a guy has a baby in WFH care,

The hospital will do everything to blame the guy. It happened to a guy and it was a nightmare.

As a guy, "hard-up" at WFH, he might think it is fun,

To be with a WFH woman, but for all the problems it could cause, he should run.

If a guy is trying to seek a good and stable woman for a wife,

Look elsewhere because WFH women will only cause him strife.

Believe me, I have been there, asked guys, "Why try?",

Because relationships at WFH are always against the guy.

# Poem #84: Ode to Advanced Placement Classes

Thanks to Advanced Placement (AP) classes I got 12 credits for college in high school,
Plus these classes helped me test through classes, like math, I am no fool.
I knew American History so good that on the AP test,
I scored so well I got college credit, that's the best.
Even though I was more of a scientist and not a literary scholar,
I got such a high score on the English AP test I got college credit, that made me holler.
I got college credit for Biology due to knowing that animals are inherently lazy,
Animals try not to waste energy, that would be crazy.
I also got college credit for American Government, that was good,
Maybe I should have went into politics, I still could!
However, I learned a lot of material in many an AP class,
That I tested out of college classes or the material helped me pass.
Due to calculus AP, I tested all the way to Multivariable Calculus and I made a roar,
Which surprised the heck out of my high school math teacher; she "hit the floor".
I did well in Spanish AP and low-and-behold,
I was shocked by the two "A" grades in college Spanish classes when the grades came out and I was told.
I did well in Computer Science in college because I learned,
Pascal then Ada for computer languages, programmed better, and better grades I earned.
Taking all those AP tests, I learned a bunch,
How college exams were like and to study in a "crunch".
Also, AP classes earned a higher GPA by a point,
Even though I did homework for many hours until I was disjoint.
Plus, AP classes, a lot of them, look good on paper,
To show a college your smart and hardworking, if going to college is your caper.
I wanted to take AP classes and put knowledge in my head,
That knowledge is still "up there" and will be there until I am dead.
AP classes helped me in college to give me many a tool,
To get a better job, that is why I did so well in school.

## Poem #85: Ode to Wearing Glasses

I wear glasses because I am legally blind,
I am so near-sighted it makes things near and far, without glasses, hard to find.
I have been wearing glasses since kindergarten in school,
Kids used to make fun of me and make me feel like a fool.
I play sports and glasses are hard to use when I sweat,
They get all slimy and it is hard to see as you can bet.
Glasses, in all precipitation, are a pain,
I cannot see and they are hard to dry-off, especially in the rain.
Glasses get in the way when I shave,
Also, I have to take them off and cannot see when I bathe.
Glasses are hard to were under goggles in chemistry class,
Especially when it is warm, but I had to deal with it or I wouldn't pass.
Glasses are also fogging up when I wear a mask,
Anybody with glasses can tell you that, all you have to do is ask.
Glasses are also a problem if anybody wearing them gets in a fight,
People will attack those glasses and blind the wearer, which just isn't right.
People belittle people with glasses as if it were a game,
To make fun of someone's handicap, have those people "no shame".
These glasses', wearing them all the time, gets old,
I also hear I look better without them, so I was told.
The worst is if the glasses get lost or broken,
Then I am blind and I am at everybody's mercy, truth be spoken.
Then people with glasses are the butt of other people's jest,
"Four Eyes" and so on are an insult, I have heard even though I try my best.
What people say to people with glasses is downright rude,
And they get offended when people with glasses give them attitude.
I just wish people would stop and the other glasses issues would get off my mind,
Because that is my "cross-to-bear" by being born legally blind.

## Poem #86: Vacations of My Life.

I cherish all the vacations of my life,
Here are some of the vacations that greatly lessened my strife.
Myrtle Beach was my favorite vacation and I am a big fan,
Even though that was the first vacation I sunburned when I went to tan.
When I went to Vermont, people drank maple syrup like coffee,
The maple syrup was too rich and thick to drink by me.
I went to West Virginia and went into a heated pool in the snow,
But when a celebrity's brother tried to sell my family timeshare it was time to go.
When I went to Gatlinburg, Tennessee, I heard many a bluegrass song,
Everybody joined in so I just sang along.
When I went to Orlando, Florida, I liked Universal Studio and Disney World a lot,
I remember doing so much that my muscles were "shot".
When I went to Miami, Florida, my dad's cousin took us to South Beach,
I learned so much because he knew how to teach.
I went to Jacksonville, Florida, where my brother called it a "suburb city",
Too bad I didn't have more time to see it. What a pity!
I went to Delaware to see my Uncle Sunny,
I remember going to a restaurant that had eggs that were extra runny.
I loved Ocean City, Maryland, where I went to both the ocean and the bay,
My family and I spent time at both beaches in one day.
I went to Pensacola, Florida, where my brother learned how to fly,
He was a Naval Aviator after he graduated from Annapolis; he is an "academy guy".
I went to Canada, where with the Boy Scouts we saw the mint,
Try not to camp too close to water because of black flies that is my hint.
I went to New York City (NYC), New York, to see my dad's cousin wed,
There was so much to do in NYC, I couldn't go to bed.
I loved going to Puerto Rico with my family and my brother's wife,
Here are some of my favorite vacations I went on in my life.

## Poem #87: Boredom in My Life

There is boredom in my life every day,
I just want something better in my life, to God I pray.
I just wish I could work, play and be free,
But I am heavily restricted by the Psychiatric Security and Review Board, the PSRB.
Due to the PSRB, I am professionally unfulfilled doing menial work,
So not only am I bored, but I have to "live off the dole" like some kind of jerk.
Due to the PSRB, I cannot go far,
And be bored because I cannot have a car.
I get bored walking around the same ground,
Due to the PSRB, I have to, around my residential living program, stick around.
I am so bored I elect to sleep and hibernate,
So I don't break any PSRB rules, so I go to bed early and not late.
To have nothing to do and be bored all the time,
For a younger person to be so restricted ought to be a crime.
Watching television after so long can be a bore,
But it is one of the few things that isn't a chore.
I even tried to learn how to cook,
Because I am so tired and bored of reading many a book.
I can't find anything to do that is fun,
So I am bored and cannot wait until the day is done.
I am so bored that I eat too much food,
"Bored Eating", because, for nothing anything I am not in the mood.
I try to do something, in which boredom I can fight,
But due to the PSRB and corona virus, I can do nothing, right?
A lot of the day I just lie in bed,
To get through the day and lessen the boredom, like I am dead.
I can tell you, to actually live and to be fulfilled; currently the way I am living is not the way,
Yet this is what I do day in and day out every day.

## Poem #88: Ode to Medication

There are plenty of medications taken by me,
From mental to physical health, to let me be.
I take **Risperdone** to keep my mental health at bay,
So I can be free of Whiting Forensic Hospital (WFH) so I can be free to work and play.
**Medformin**, I lake to keep my blood sugar in check,
Because I am a diabetic due to **Risperdone**. What the heck!
I also take **Tradjenta** to keep my blood sugar down,
Even though I watch what I eat when I eat "on the town".
I have to take **Vitamin D** pills because I don't get enough sun,
Because I am in the house and, due to the Psychiatric Security and Review Board (PSRB), can't go outside for fun.
I take **Colace** so I can bear,
My poop not being constipated. Without **Colace** it is a nightmare.
I take an **Omega 3** which is a large pill,
It takes up most of my medication box when I fill.
I take **Aspirin** for my heart,
To help against heart attacks. I haven't had one so it must do its part.
I take **Simvastatin** to keep my cholesterol good,
I take it every day and not eat grapefruit, like I should.
I take **Fenofibrate** for things like triglycerides and fat,
I take it for physical health needs and "that is that".
I take **Tylenol** for a PRN for pain,
Because I have headaches so bad its insane.
I take **Mylanta** as a PRN when I have heartburn,
I need to sleep, despite the heartburn, and sleep I yearn.
I took **Cialis** for erectile dysfunction for awhile,
But insurance doesn't cover it, so my penis does not get erect like a file.
All of these medications, I take daily and wish I was free,
To not be "chained" to these medications, taken twice a day, morning and/or night, by me.

## Poem #89: My Favorite Dinners

I have my favorite dinners that I like to eat,
Funny enough my favorite dinners all have meat.
I only had Beef Wellington once,
It was wonderful, but I was at a fancy restaurant, so I hope I didn't look like a dunce.
I love pulled pork with barbeque sauce on a bun,
I like to put coleslaw in the sandwich too, just for fun.
Seafood Paella is a treat for me,
Last time I had it, I shared it with my family.
Hamburgers, I like them for dinner all the time,
I have had them with "everything", including bacon, but with peanut butter is a crime.
Hot dogs, I like because they are an easily prepared food,
I like to put onions, relish, and mayonnaise on them to give them attitude.
Surf and Turf for dinner I like shrimp and steak,
I also like it with potatoes prepared by mash or bake.
Mofongo with shrimp is a dinner delight,
To have this Puerto Rican favorite makes my night.
I like Meat Lovers Pizza for dinner from Pizza Hut,
Especially with pan pizza crust, to not like it, I would be a nut.
Ribs, either pork or beef, I like when the meat falls of the bone,
I like to eat them by myself, to enjoy them all alone.
I like veal parmesan as an Italian dinner dish,
I always want more. Oh I wish!
I like clams casino, especially made by a skilled hand,
Clams casino needs that skill because without it you might get some unwanted sand.
I like chili for dinner when it gets cold,
I like it with rice and corn in it, so you have been told!
I like to eat these meals for dinner until I am replete,
For these are my favorite dinners I like to eat.

## Poem #90: Not Being Allowed to Drive a Car

I am not allowed to drive a car because of the Psychiatric Security and Review Board, the PSRB.

This really restricts my ability to be free.

I am really restricted to places near rather than far,

Because I am not allowed to drive or ride in an unauthorized car.

I cannot go to many places to eat,

Because I have to walk to the restaurant for a treat.

I cannot even have a license because the PSRB doesn't care,

The PSRB expect blind obedience, which for me, is a nightmare.

Without being able to go anywhere new, my life is a bore,

And this makes getting through life a hefty chore.

I have to even walk to my weekly appointments and can't be late,

Even in the extreme hot and cold, this makes me irate.

I cannot get a more prominent job and work,

So I have to stay at home, without a car, and feel like a "jerk".

Due to the PSRB's control over me has no reason or rhyme,

I have to be held punitively without a car, which should be a crime.

Even with all of these restrictions I cannot give attitude,

Because the PSRB will write a bad report with the "power of the pen" and I won't be able be discharged and get a car if I am rude.

Not being able to enjoy a nice car ride is wrong,

But I have no real legal representation to battle the PSRB, so with these oppressive restrictions I must go along.

I like driving because I feel like I can "fly",

Freedom and seeing new things keeps the "luster in my eye".

However, the PSRB has their rules and have spoken,

That I cannot have a car and I will go to Whiting Forensic Hospital (WFH) if their rules are broken.

Without a car to enjoy life, my life is lame,

And I am just caught up in the PSRB's game.

As you can see the freedom of a car is precious to me,

But my life was all taken away by the dictatorial PSRB.

## Poem #91: I Like Military History

My favorite subject I liked was military history,
It was my favorite hobby to be researched by me.
I used to get its magazine and I was glad to pay,
To read about military history every day.
I especially liked to read about ancient military history. Why?
Because back then militaries had to fight hand-to-hand with sound tactics or die.
I liked to read about legendary battles and fights of yore,
Military historians had compiled all of its legendary lore.
I liked military leaders, who used traps and bait,
The enemy into attacking because the enemy military leaders just had no patience and could not wait.
Reading about military leaders who used their advantages to pound,
Their opponent's armies into the ground.
Reading about military leaders using horses, tanks, and all types of armored car,
To affect the mobility and availability of military assets on battlefields away and far.
Reading about military leader's tactics to cut the enemy deep,
So the power and monetary rewards the winner could reap.
Reading about interchangeable parts developed by military leaders to repair,
Their armies fast, so fast that for an unexpecting opponent it is a nightmare.
Learning that militaries developed prepackaged food,
So military leaders could keep their armies marching and ready for fighting by keeping them "in the mood".
 Learning about military leader's style and how they deployed their army's might,
So they could beat their enemies and dominate the fight.
To read about past armies and how they managed their danger,
From fighting armies that used different tactics from which their opponents were a stranger.
For the glory for the "conquering" military leaders that won,
Those leaders are forever revered in history as an awesome person.
Heck, it took a lot of military leaders for me to be free,
To write this poem and honor their contributions to military history.

## Poem #92: Ode to My Favorite Side Dishes

When it comes to side dishes, to the entrée, they mean more,
From this list of these side dishes, I think they are "hardcore".
For macaroni and cheese, I love all that gooey cheese,
To be melted all over the macaroni, oh it is a tease!
Green bean casserole with a covering that has a crunch,
It is definitely a tasty side dish I like to have for lunch.
Sweet potato casserole with marshmallows and brown sugar is a tasty treat,
I like its consistency and the fact that its sweet.
I like cream corn as a sweet and creamy food,
When I get it, I think I am a lucky dude.
With baked beans, I like almost any flavor,
With a smooth consistency and the taste that I savor.
Macaroni salad is creamy and I think tastes great,
But due to the pasta I have to worry about gaining weight.
Mashed potatoes, I like with cheese, garlic, or butter,
It is wonderful, no other words I have to utter.
French fries are a good side dish crunchy and golden brown,
To eat them all, to my stomach, they are going down!
I like nothing more than having garlic bread,
There is nothing more I like with an Italian meal instead.
Collard Greens with pieces of meat have their place,
They are a big part of the meal, not just taking up space.
From my Hispanic heritage, there is nothing as nice,
As having a good side dish or red beans and rice.
Steamed broccoli is healthier than the rest,
But ranks right up there as a great side dish, one of the best
The best things about these side dishes are that they are available at the grocery store,
Because these side dishes accentuate the entrée and I want more.

## Poem #93: Ode to Groups

I have many psychosocial groups to attend almost ever day,
Some are therapeutic or more entertaining with their own things to say.
One of my favorite groups is movie group,
All of us get together, have a snack, and watch a movie with the whole troop.
Mental Models is a group to figure out how the mind does work,
To understand everything from why we, as humans, do things to why a person is a jerk.
Bring it, Grill it is a group where the staff cooks the food,
On a grill, so the group can eat and interact without being rude.
Bingo group is a group where we play Bingo for fun,
And people also get prizes for every Bingo they won.
Dialelectic Behavioral Therapy (DBT) helps people be mindful at the time,
To think other than "black or white", so the group's members don't do something bad like commit a crime.
Better Days, the group reads from a book and answers questions three,
To help keep a better outlook on life and live more worry-free.
Coping strategies group helps with issues so deep,
To give ways to work through things do its members don't lose sleep.
Me and my mental health group we learn about illnesses of the mind,
To try to help deal with our mental illness and find peace that is hard to find.
Positive thinking group helps to try to see the good,
So you "spin" things and "reframe" them in a positive light, so I am not always "knocking on wood".
Food and Nutrition group, the group learns what is good to eat,
The group also tries to get healthy foods, which is a treat.
Men's group, the group learns how men think and how we get through life,
The members learn things like roles, rules, and even how to deal with an unruly wife.
Live life laughing group, the members tell jokes and "learn" to laugh,
And the members watch videos of comedians who talk about many a human gaff.
All these groups, my boredom they take away,
Because they show me new things to learn every day.

## Poem #94: How I Would Love to Win the Lottery

I would love to win the lottery and win lots of money,
I bet winning would make my days a lot more "sunny".
If I won the lottery I would "hit the floor",
As for my job, I would be heading for the door.
I would hire somebody to drive my car,
To drive me around, both near and far.
I would hire a chef to make me good meals to eat,
I would hire a chef that is very competent in cooking meat.
I would always be happy and in a good mood,
If I won the lottery, then there would be no reason to be rude.
I would go on wonderful trips with nor reason or rhyme,
I would enjoy being me, on my own schedule, all of the time.
I would relax and enjoy myself and feel, overall, great,
And if I wanted to I would sleep in and stay up late.
I would get things like a nice and decent house,
And with a prenuptial, I would also get a nice and decent spouse.
I would do things I wanted to and grow old,
Experience the best of the world, as I am told.
I would enjoy going to many a sports game,
And live the "good life" instead of a life that is lame.
I would get science things accomplished and done,
Because I am a research scientist and I think science is fun.
I would like to take some time and hone my gemstone-fabricating art,
With my ceramics materials research, I can make gemstones from the heart.
I would spend more time answering the question, "Why?",
And enjoy answering this question until the day I die.
Winning the lottery, oh wouldn't it be funny,
To live life grand and not have to worry about money.

## Poem #95: My Favorite Number, Four

For all my life, my favorite number is four,
It is my favorite number, no less and no more.
I like that I can count to four in one hand,
Four used to be common to see in a rock band.
In math, the Cartesian plane has four quadrants in a graph sheet,
Learning how to graph different lines and shapes, I could not beat.
There are four arms and legs appendages on a woman or man,
These four appendages are so useful, so I am a fan.
Some animals have four legs to walk and run,
They need all four to efficiently move, they cannot only use one.
Humans and some animals have four fingers to use,
To grip things or use certain tools, these humans and animals cannot afford a finger to lose.
There are four quarters in a dollar to make correct change,
Since quarters are useful for things like parking meters, this, governmental officials, cannot easily rearrange.
Cars have four tires to make them go,
Four-wheel-drive helps certain cars get around in the snow.
A bedroom, a bathroom, hallway, and kitchen is about a minimum for a house,
This is four rooms that people and their mate, at a minimum, needs to clean if person has a spouse.
Four Square is a common kids game,
With four squares to move the ball into, more or less would be lame.
Connect Four is a game where a person needs to get four of your color chips in a row unbroken,
So the winner can say, "Connect Four!" and win after these words are spoken.
In a day, some people have three meals and a snack,
That is four times eating if you, the reader, is keeping track.
A family unit usually has four members on shows on TV,
With one father, one mother, one sister, and one brother on their family tree.
In the end, I am not ever sore,
Because my favorite number is the number four.

# Poem #96: Ode to Cleaning My Bathroom

Cleaning the bathroom is a lot of work to take off all of the grime,
Not to mention I have to clean it all of the time.
If the bathroom isn't clean, then it will get covered in ick,
This will grow mold and bacteria that will make the house inhabitants sick.
I clean the toilet every day,
Because a nasty toilet tells a lot about a person in a negative way.
I daily clean the shower,
So the bathroom does not look nasty and smell sour.
I daily have to clean the bathroom sink,
Because of the poor drainage, it will get nasty, what a fink!
It is important to scrub out where I bathe,
And it is equally important to cleanup where I shave.
I also daily sweep and mop the floor,
I also do my best to cleanup all the hair that gets trapped behind the door.
The towel I dry of with I put in the laundry when it is all-around,
Starting to look nasty, I don't want it to look as if I dragged it on the ground.
I clean my bathroom a lot because as a guy,
I don't want to follow a dirty stereotype, that is why I try,
To make sure it is clean of hair because I shed,
Like a dog, and the alternative looks bad instead.
I usually cleanup at night,
Because I want everything clean for the next day, which is right.
I even clean out the excess hair from my comb,
Because I want a neat and tidy home.
I think all of this cleaning is smart,
Because I have less chance of being sick from the very start.
I try to clean routinely not to buildup bathroom slime,
From all of the bathroom "funk" and its subsequent grime.

## Poem #97: The Whiting Forensic Hospital (WFH) Staff Abuse Their Patients

The Whiting Forensic Hospital (WFH) staff abused their patients every day,
But no adequate legal resources and lack or press coverage lead to patients' dismay.
I was physically abused by a staff, number of times, five,
The first time I did not even have glasses and I am legally blind, I am lucky to be alive.
The WFH staff would treat the patients worse than sheep,
They would be "jack-asses" while supposedly "treating us", they act, collectively, like a creep.
The WFH staff would go ahead and pound,
Patients they did not like, that act up, into the ground.
The WFH staff would "pay" certain patients like a whore,
To attack patients they did not like, so the staff could further attack the patient after the victim were knocked to the floor.
The WFH staff would aggressively address a patient as bait,
To try to get the patient to "go off" so they could bet overtime for constant observation (CO) working late.
I saw a WFH staff, during a "code", hit a patient in the neck,
The patient was seriously hurt and could not breathe what the heck!
I also saw WFH staff, eating patient's food,
Especially grapes, so us patients could not get any, how rude!
WFH staff would take "cheap shots" in a fight,
Hitting male patients below the belt, treatment? Yeah right!
WFH staff saw other staff doing patients wrong,
Yet there is "honor amongst thieves" so they just play along.
WFH staff really did not care,
If a patient did a good thing, then a bad thing they reported to the patient's nightmare.
Most WFH staff did not even know their patient's name,
They found it easier to attack and negatively report on an unnamed patient, what a shame!
I saw a couple staff circle a patient and punch,
The patient so hard I could hear an audible, "Crunch!".
At WFH, that was just the way,
The staff behaved towards patients every day.

## Poem #98: Ode to Sending Cards By Mail

I enjoy getting a card in the mail,
My eyes "light up" when I see the unopened card without fail.
I don't just get a card in the mail every day,
The cards I get are for special occasions or when somebody has something to say.
When I get a card in a mail I feel like a star,
Especially if it is sent by a family member who lives afar.
I enjoy a card that is picked for me all-around,
Instead of an impersonalized email, which I get "by the pound".
I enjoy a message and a card that is picked by someone I know,
Not just a random computer screen with words written "on the go".
I understand the "personality" of a card specifically picked for me,
And not some generalized mass-email sent for the world to see.
A paper card gives me emotions so deep,
That in happiness or in sorrow I just may weep.
Even as simple as a paper card to say "Hi!",
Makes me happy enough for my heart to "fly".
A card by mail can make my heart repair,
After a tragedy, to know somebody does care.
A card by mail for my birthday is very fun,
Makes me feel good, like a person who was in a race and won.
A card by mail sent for serious or for jest,
Can validate my feelings without a request.
Even just a simple card sent by mail "off the rack",
Can make me feel like somebody "has my back".
Cards in the mail, in my heart, have a place,
And I hang on to them because I cherish them and not because they take-up space.
I can look at my old cards, that keep a trail,
Of special memories that I still remember because of paper cards in the mail.

## Poem #99: My Favorite Boy Scout Merit Badges

When I was a Boy Scout, I made it all the way to Eagle Scout.

Merit badges and having fun earning them was what it was all about.

Small Boat Sailing, I learned how to us the jib and main sail,

And earned that merit badge without fail.

Camping, I had to go on camping trips and make and break camp,

This was harder to do when rained and everything was damp.

Swimming, I learned to do when I was young,

When I earned the merit badge a bell, at the pool, we had rung.

First Aid, I practiced bandaging on another scout's leg and arm,

To learn how to help somebody if they come into harm.

Citizenship in the Nation, I learned about why it is important to vote,

For all my ancestors who came over by plane or boat.

Lifesaving, I had to lift, out of the water, a weight,

To simulate a person, who needed help quick and could not wait.

Environmental Science, I had to investigate nature in the woods,

To see how nature interacted with humans and how people got "natural goods".

Shotgun Shooting, I shot 47 out of 50 pigeons of clay,

To earn that merit badge made my day.

Canoeing, I had trouble trying to get back in the canoe,

After hours of trying, I figured ot what to do.

Rowing was the "easiest" of the boating merit badges and I did not lose sleep,

I just rowed the boat well without a peep.

Indian Lore, I learned about Native Americans and learned how to Indian Dance,

But I wasn't that good, but I would try again if I had the chance.

Leatherwork, I used leather to make works of art,

That I gave to family and friends, "straight from the heart".

I earned so many merit badges that on my sash I could tout,

That I learned many things being a Boy Scout.

# Poem #100: With Regards to My Style of Poetry

I worked hard on my poetry style for this poetry book,
To be so personal with my poetry, I was so scared I shook.
I introduced rules to my poetry imposed by me,
I like my poems more regimented than free.
Every two lines had to rhyme,
To find words about the topic and did rhyme took a lot of skill and a lot of time.
I like the first two lines to rhyme with the last two lines at the poem's end,
I even let the first and last line use the same words, which is not a rule, just ended up being a trend.
I used a lot of poems that used two line pairings as a list,
Those poems were fun to write, but hurt my wrist.
I used a lot of poems to talk about serious topics to "pack a punch",
Because these poems were about my life and experiences and there were bad times, a bunch.
I wrote a few poems about my family and our home,
And I also wrote poems about experiences where I roam.
I tried not to use lines that were similar or the same,
Because I thought repeating lines was boring and kind of lame.
I had to write "sticky notes" to what I wanted to put in poems on paper,
To try and write the best poems for this poetry book's caper.
I did my best to write the best poems I could,
Hopefully the topics and rhymes were very good.
Some of these poems showed I am a little old,
By the topics, rhymes, and words I used in the poems, I was told.
These poems let my stress out and lessened my overall strife,
And got me out of my "humdrum" life.
I am proud of what I wrote and I liked to share,
For topics I wrote about and for these subjects I did care.
These poems had a reasonable time to write it took,
For me to share my life and my poetry style in this poetry book.